LIFE & DEATH OF A HIGHLAND HOTEL
A PHOTOGRAPHIC ESSAY

JAMES CARRON

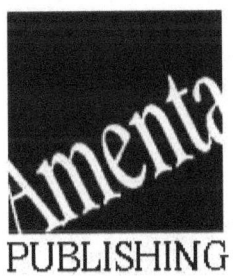

Amenta Publishing

www.amenta.ink

LIFE & DEATH OF A HIGHLAND HOTEL
A PHOTOGRAPHIC ESSAY

By James Carron

First published 2017 by Amenta Publishing

Copyright © James Carron 2017

ISBN 9781976566479

The right of James Carron to be identified as the author of this work has been asserted by him in accordance with the Copyright, Designs and Patents Act 1988.

All rights reserved. No part of this publication may be reproduced, stored in a retrieval system, or transmitted in any form, or by any means, electronic, mechanical, photocopying, recording or otherwise, without permission in writing from the publisher.

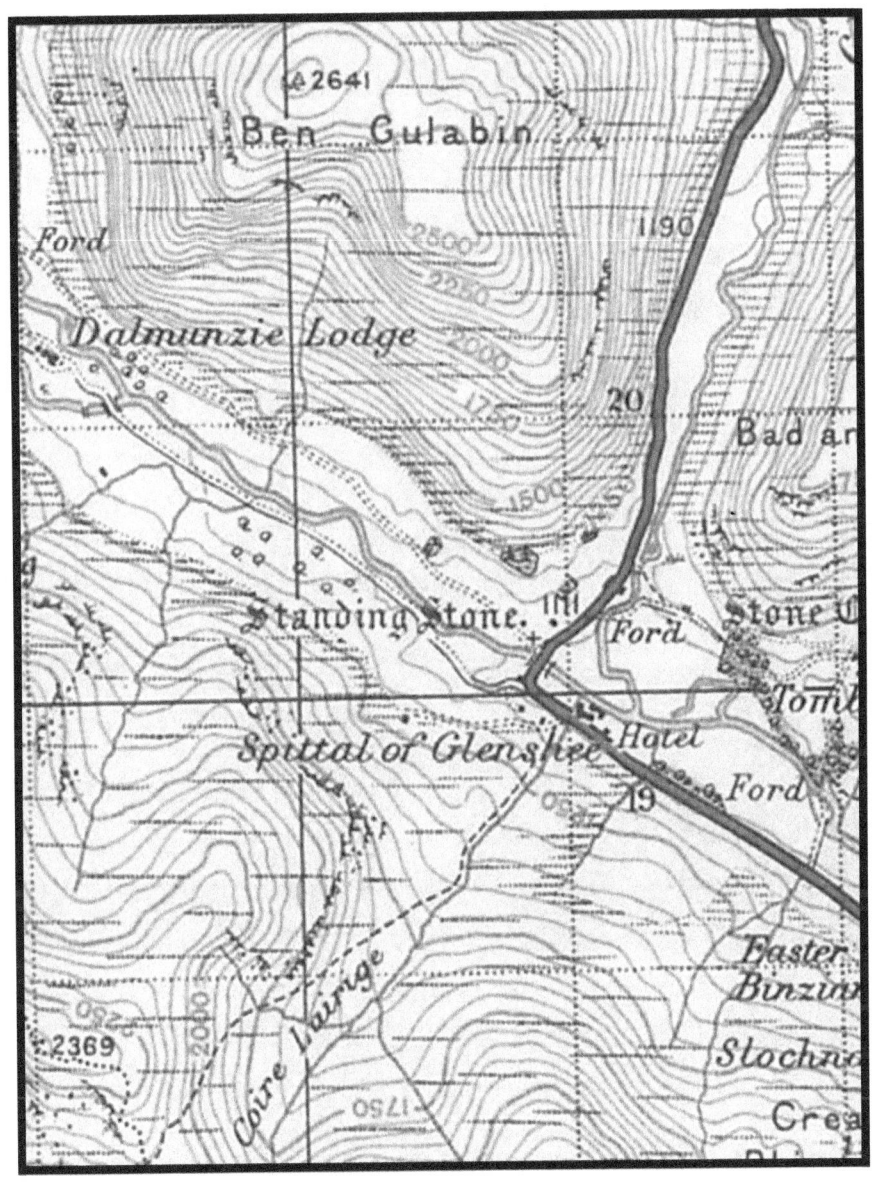

Every journey starts with a map...

BLAIRGOWRIE,
The Switzerland of Scotland.

Why not Stay at

SPITTAL HOTEL,
Spittal of Glenshee
(1,100 feet above sea-level).

20 miles from Blairgowrie. Second to none for Cuisine, Service, Comfort, and Cleanliness. Fresh butter, cream, eggs, and other produce daily from our own two farms.

Free trout fishing on Lochs and River Shee; free shooting over 600 acres of moorland.

Garage, Petrol, Oil. Up-to-date Cars for Hire.

We cater weekly for Cook's Tourists.

We can cater for you.

Write for terms to—

A. GRANT, Proprietor.

Telegrams—Hotel, Glenshee.

...and ends with a place to sleep.

The Spittal

Spittal of Glenshee has long been a sanctuary for weary wanderers. The Scots word 'spittal' describes a hospice or shelter for travellers, usually in mountainous country, and the outpost in Glen Shee was established in AD 941 by monks from the Cistercian monastery in Coupar Angus, 25 miles to the south.

What started life as a basic refuge on a long and lonely road through the glen evolved into a hotel proper in 1796 when the Invercauld Arms Hotel opened its doors. Owned by the Invercauld Estate, the hotel and adjoining farm were leased to various tenants over the years and, in time, the business became known as the Spittal Hotel.

In the early years of the 20th century, the hotel offered guests the pick of 20 bedrooms, a coffee room, smoking room and dining room. It could stable 20 horses and had facilities for those travelling by motor coach or car.

The hotel was popular with well-healed guests who spent weeks at a time resident in Glen Shee shooting and fishing. A nine-hole golf course was added to the attractions in 1895.

As motoring became more widespread, the hotel enjoyed the patronage of car owners and coach tours, its BP pumps an opportunity to fill up before drivers tackled the notorious Devil's Elbow, a double hairpin bend with gradients of up to 1 in 3 on the highest public road in Britain, the A93 over the Cairnwell Pass.

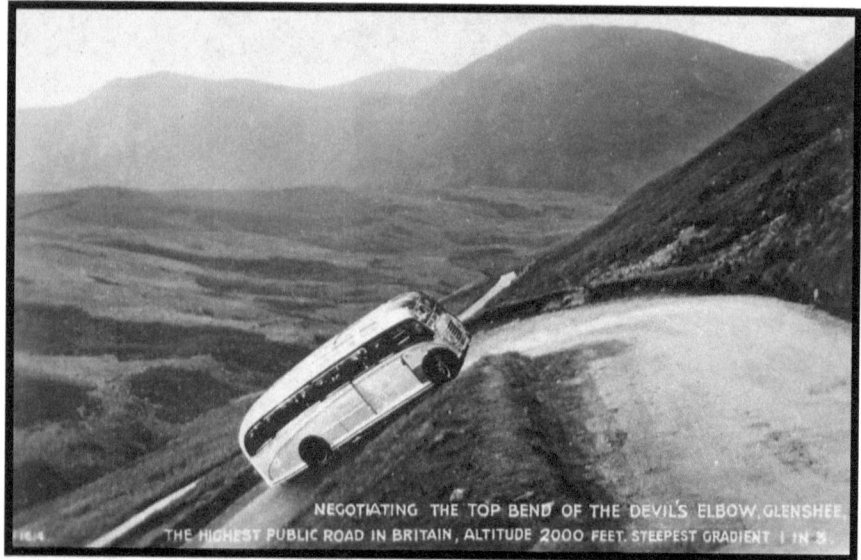

NEGOTIATING THE TOP BEND OF THE DEVIL'S ELBOW, GLENSHEE THE HIGHEST PUBLIC ROAD IN BRITAIN, ALTITUDE 2000 FEET. STEEPEST GRADIENT 1 IN 3.

The Automobile Association maintained a supply of water at the top of the Devil's Elbow so drivers could cool their often over-heated engines while buses frequently had to off-load passengers on the way up the hill in order to make it to the top.

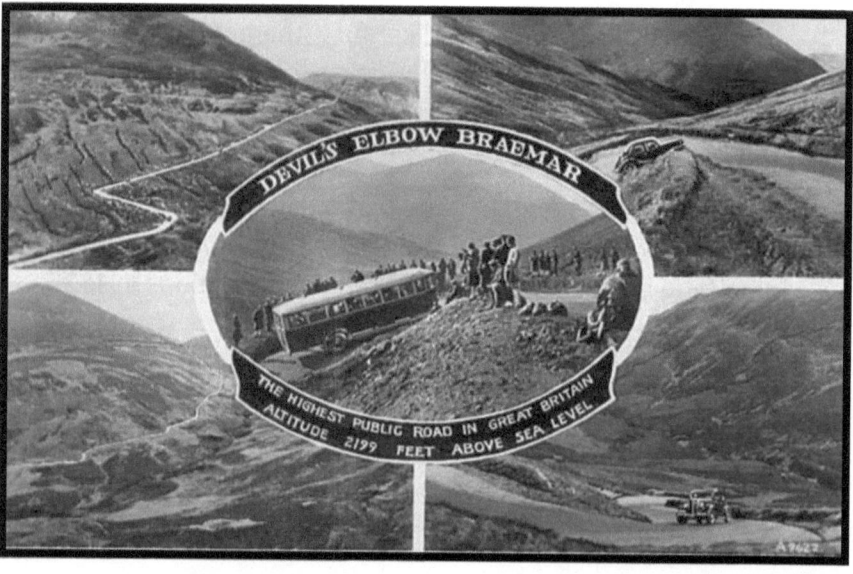

DEVIL'S ELBOW BRAEMAR
THE HIGHEST PUBLIC ROAD IN GREAT BRITAIN ALTITUDE 2199 FEET ABOVE SEA LEVEL

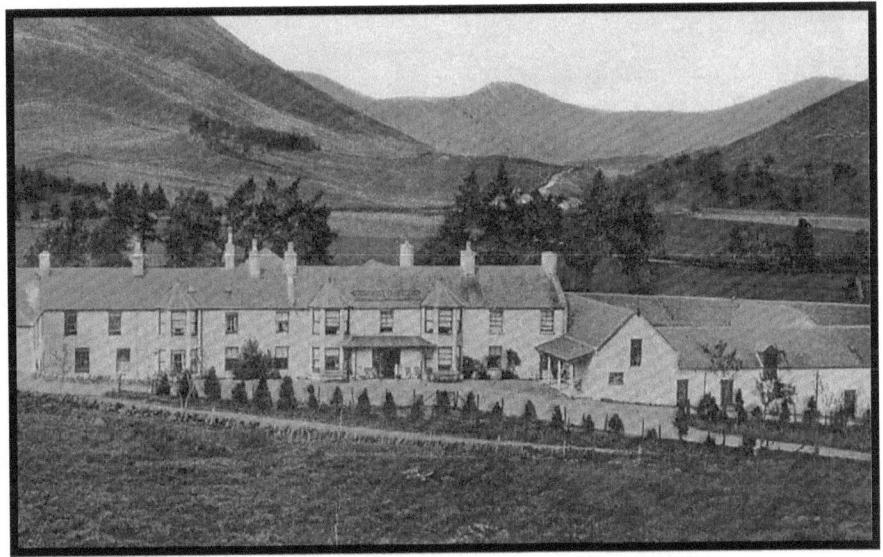

Early postcard images of the Invercauld Arms, also known as the Spittal Hotel, the one below taken in the 1930s

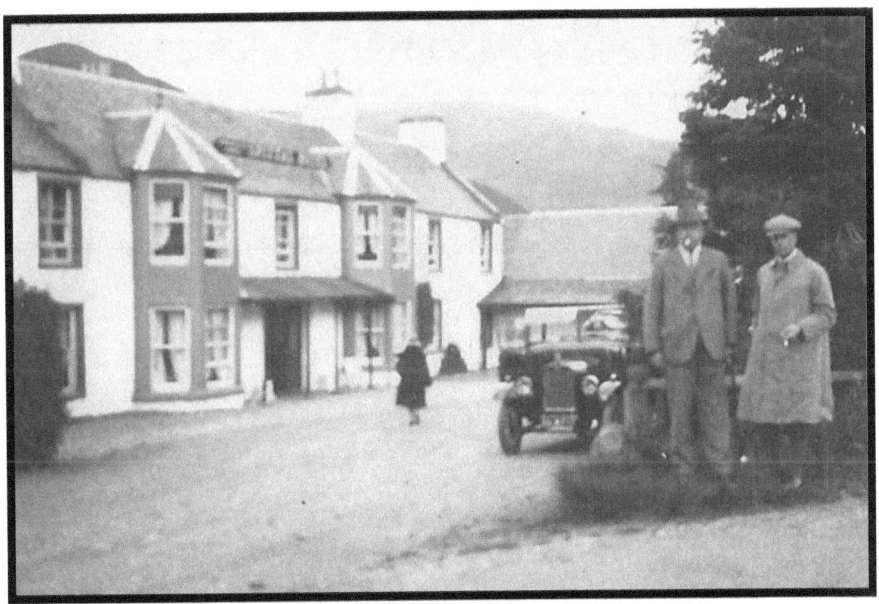

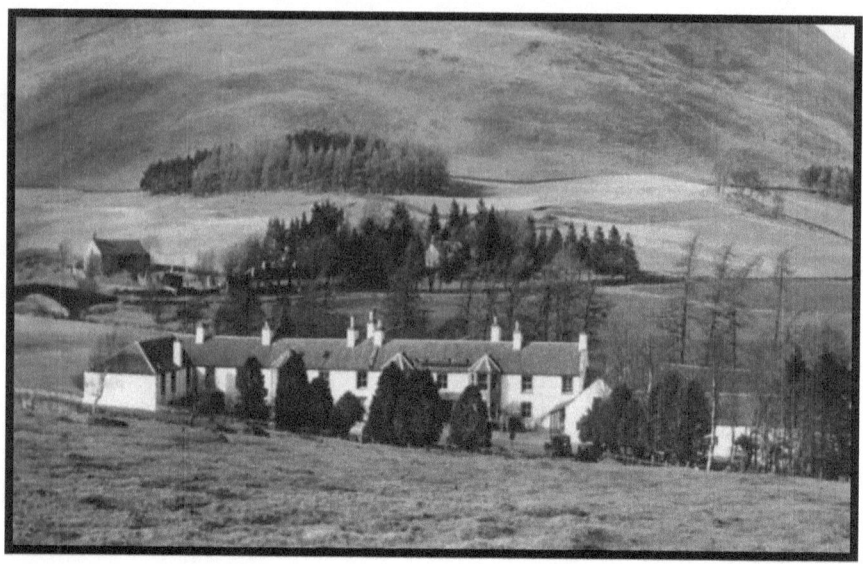

The first Spittal Hotel (above and below) appeared on numerous early postcards

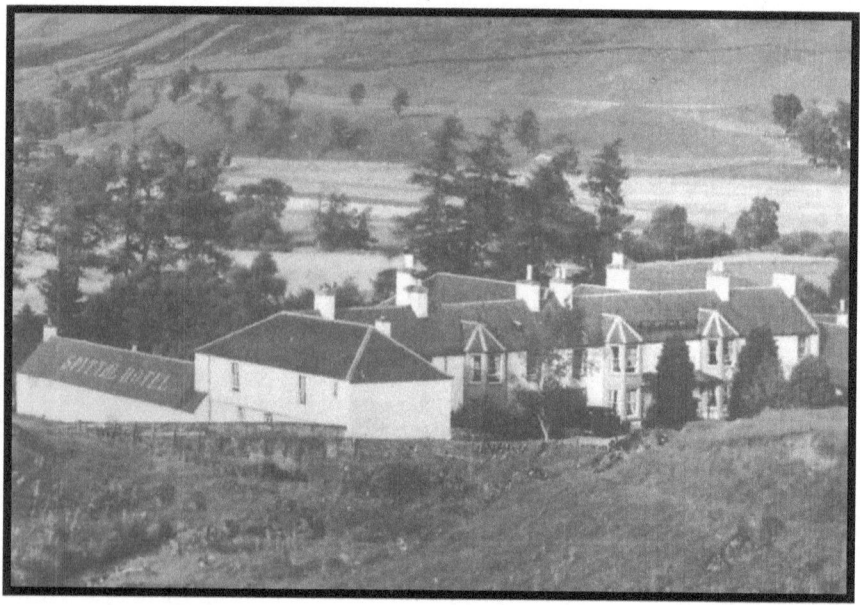

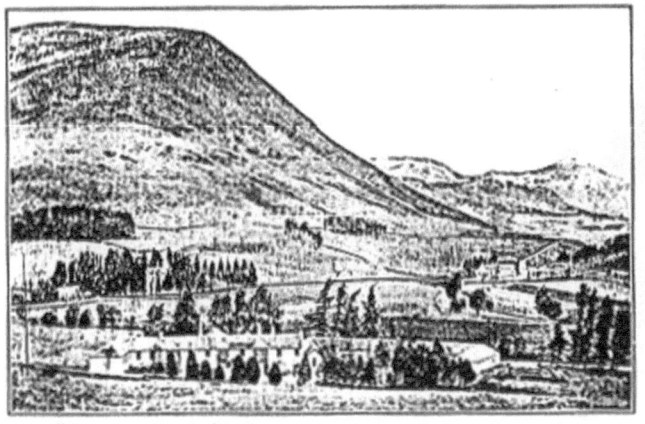

INVERCAULD ARMS &
SPITTAL HOTEL, GLENSHEE
BLAIRGOWRIE

Telegrams:—Hotel, Glenshee.   Station—Blairgowrie, 20 miles.
A. GRANT, Proprietor.

THIS famous old residential Hotel has all the glamour of remote times, yet has kept thoroughly up-to-date in service and outlook. It is modernly equipped, and stands at the head of the glen on a position 1125 feet above sea level, amidst some of the finest mountain scenery in Scotland. To sportsmen, tourists, and those in search of a restful holiday THE SPITTAL HOTEL offers unrivalled advantages.

RECOMMENDED HOTEL OF A.A. AND SCOTTISH TRAVEL ASSOCIATION.

Member of the Hotels' and Restaurants' Association of Great Britain.

DISTANCES FROM SPITTAL HOTEL.

Ballater,	31½ miles.
Balmoral,	23 miles.
Blairgowrie,	20 miles.
Kirkmichael,	13 miles.
Glenisla,	11 miles.
Alyth,	23 miles.
Reekie Linn,	18 miles.
Tulchan,	9 miles.
Perth,	35 miles.
Kirriemuir,	26 miles.
Beech Hedges,	18 miles.
Devil's Elbow,	5 miles.
Loch Vrotachan,	6 miles.
Loch Callater,	16 miles.
Loch Nan Ean,	7 miles.
Glen Tatnach,	3 miles.
Braemar,	15 miles.

FREE FISHING ON LOCHS AND RIVERS.

Loch Vrotachan.
Loch Nan Ean (May to July)
Loch Bennie (2 days a week)
The Rivers Shee and Beag.

Free shooting over 600 Acres of Hill Ground.

MOTOR GARAGE AND PETROL SUPPLIES, &c.

TARIFF OF CHARGES

Bedrooms from	5/6
Double Bedroom from	9/- to 12/-
Sitting Rooms from	7/6 to 10/- per day
Breakfast,	3/6
Lunch,	3/6
Tea (with Jams, Fresh Butter, Scones, Bread and Butter, Cakes, etc.),	1/6
Dinner,	5/-

EN PENSION TERMS—

June,	£4 4/- per week.
July,	£4 7/6 per week.
August,	£5 per week.
September,	£4 7/6 per week.
October to May,	£3 10/- per week.

NOTE.—In winter months the Hotel is heated in Corridors with stoves and made thoroughly comfortable.

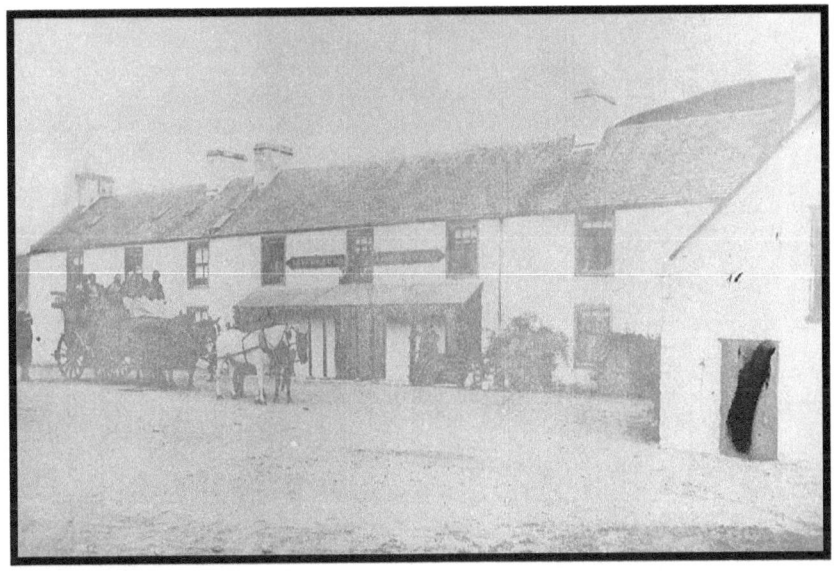

'Formerly a stage on the great military road from Perth to Fort George, it was a halting place for refreshment of the Queen and Prince Albert, on the earliest occasions of their journeying to and from Balmoral (1848); and it has a good inn.'

Ordnance Gazetteer of Scotland, 1882

'The inn at the spittle of Glen Shee is a sad one; some people do sleep at it, particularly gentlemen who go to the Highlands for shooting. I should shudder a little with disgust, were I obliged to pass a night at the Inn in Glen Shee.'

A Companion and Useful Guide to the Beauties of Scotland by Sarah Murray, 1810

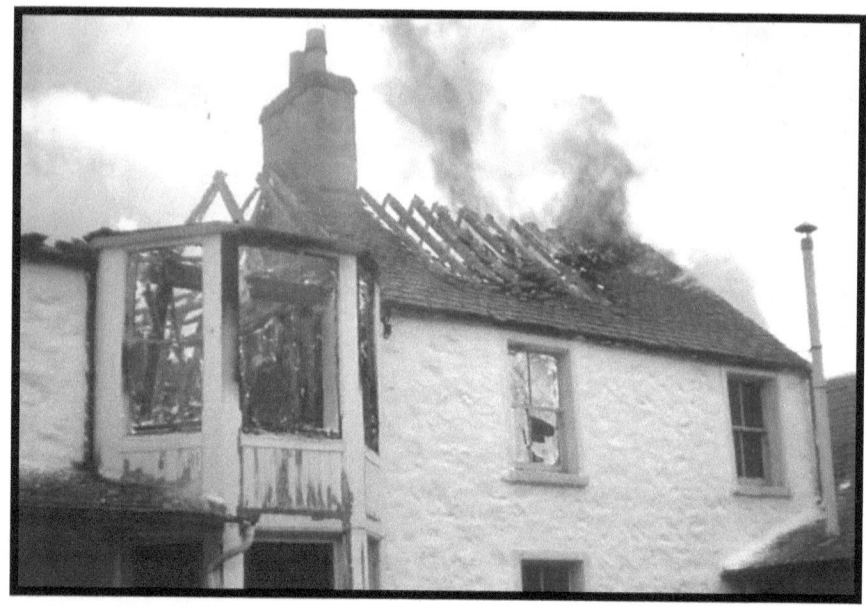

In 1957, a workman stripping paint from the roof of the building sparked a fire that destroyed the original Spittal Hotel.

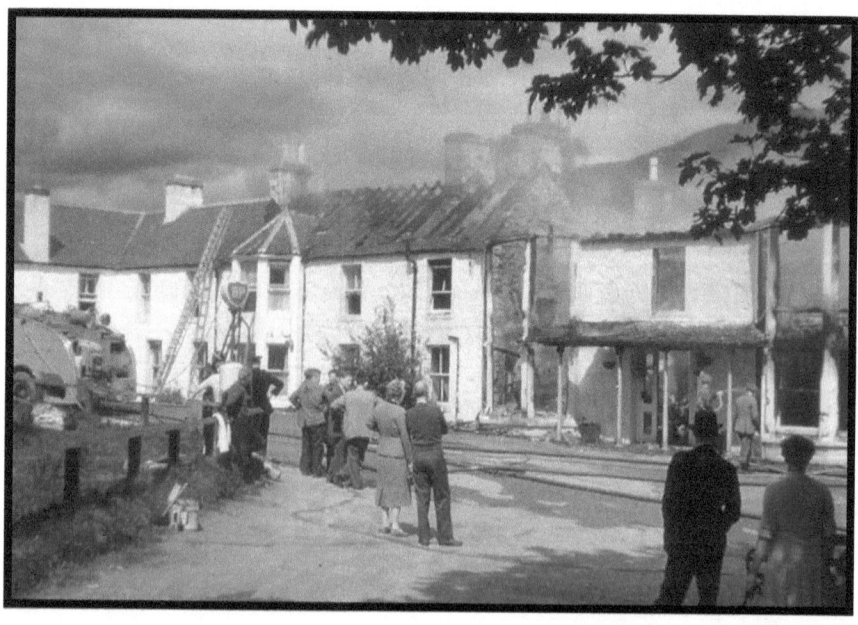

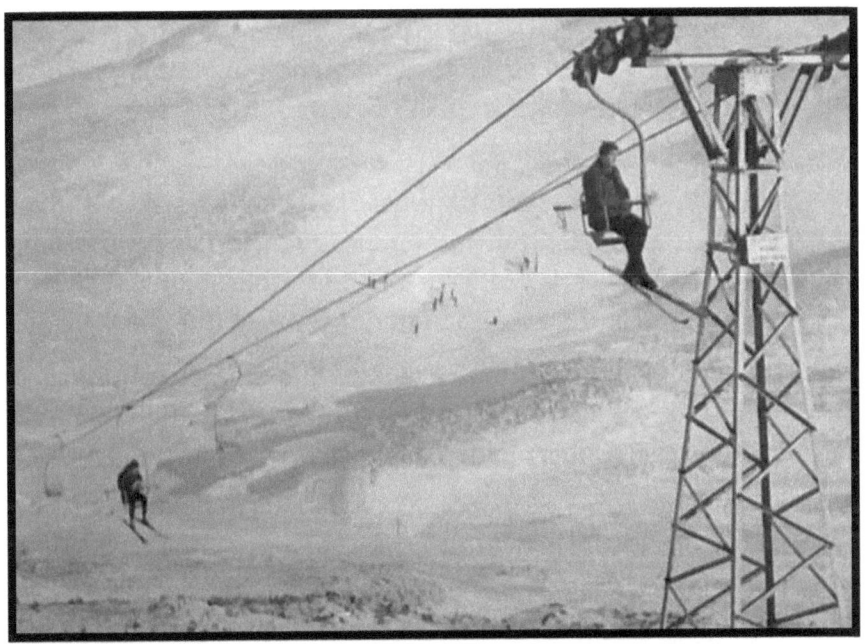

The Cairnwell Chairlift (above) and the new café at Glenshee (below)

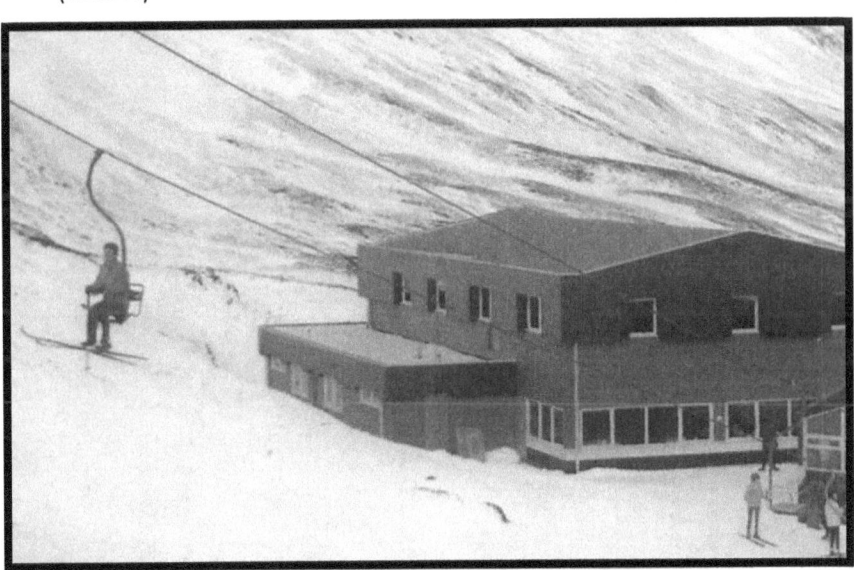

The arrival of the ski industry brought new visitors to the glen. Inspired by visits to Continental mountain resorts, Scottish pioneers of the sport started to explore the slopes of Glen Shee in the early 1930s.

In 1948, members of Dundee Ski Club, who based their activities at the Spittal Hotel, built a hut in the col between Ben Gulabin and Creagan Bheithe and later erected a mechanised tow on the shoulder of Creagan Bheithe.

The club's attentions, however, quickly turned to the higher ground of the Cairnwell and, in 1957, it built the first T-bar tow on Meall Odhar.

Forming the Glenshee Chairlift Company Ltd, the club leased land from Invercauld Estate, erected the Cairnwell Chairlift and a small café and, in 1962, opened the slopes to the public.

Over the years, Glenshee expanded into the largest ski centre in the country with 21 lifts and tows spread over four mountains and three valleys.

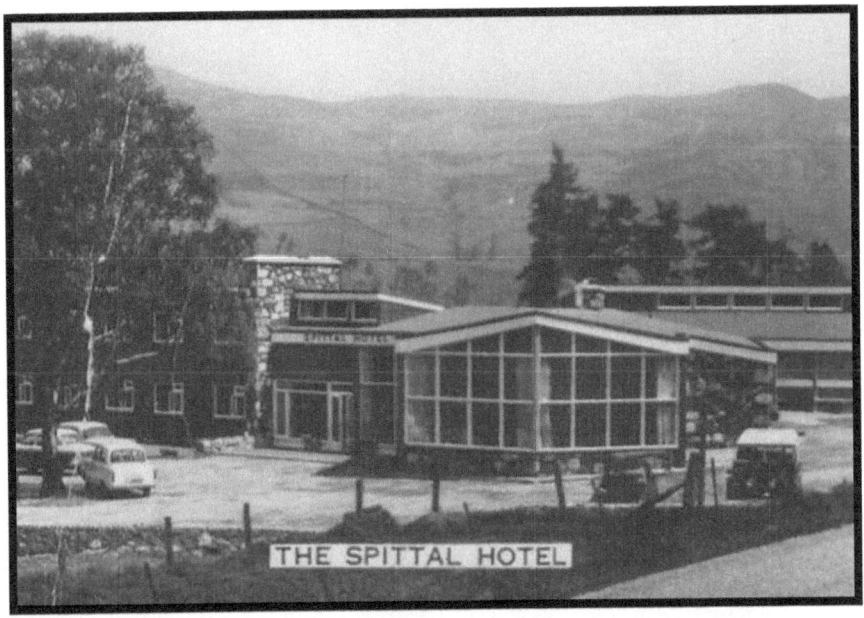

Following the untimely demise of the Spittal Hotel, a new company, Spittal of Glenshee Hotel Ltd, was set up in 1958 to redevelop the site. What remained of the original structure was demolished and a new, modern Scandinavian-style hotel rose from the ashes in the early 1960s.

Bright and airy, it incorporated a restaurant, shop and bar. There were fuel pumps at the front, car parks to either side and, to the rear, a three-storey, wooden-clad accommodation block.

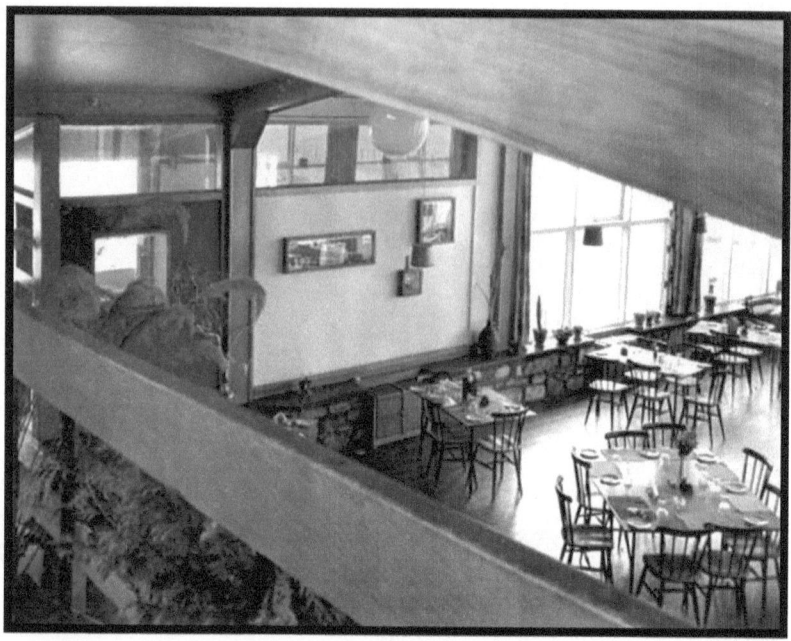

The sleek modern interior (above and below) of the 1960s Spittal of Glenshee Hotel

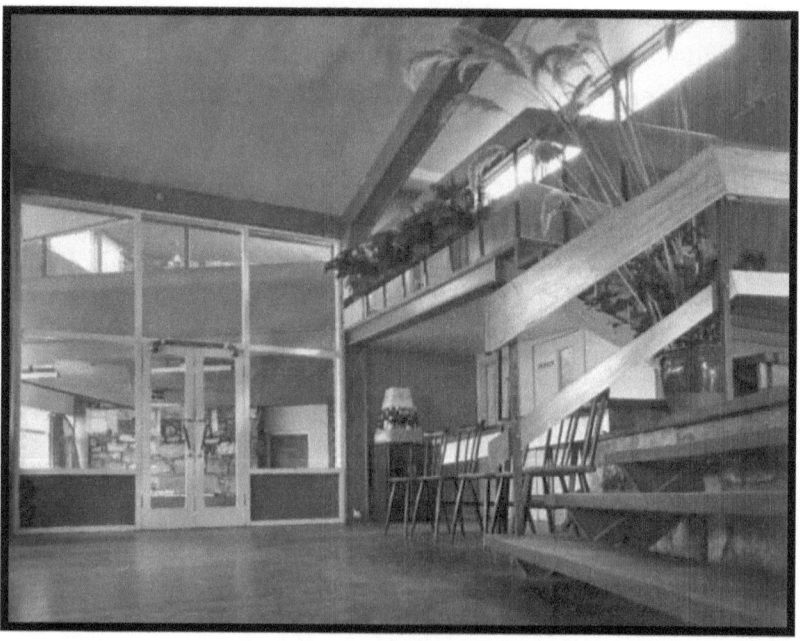

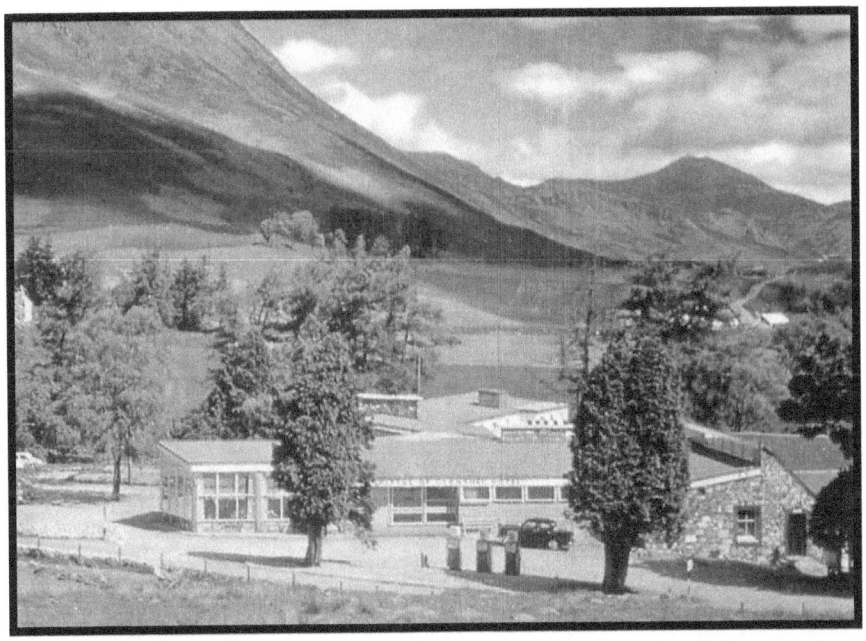

Postcard images of the new Spittal of Glenshee Hotel, showing the petrol pumps (above) and a touring coach (below)

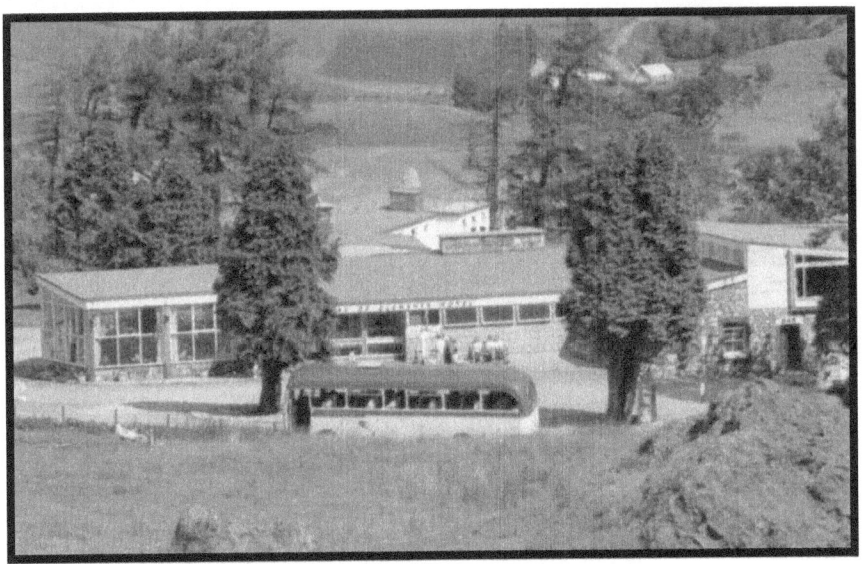

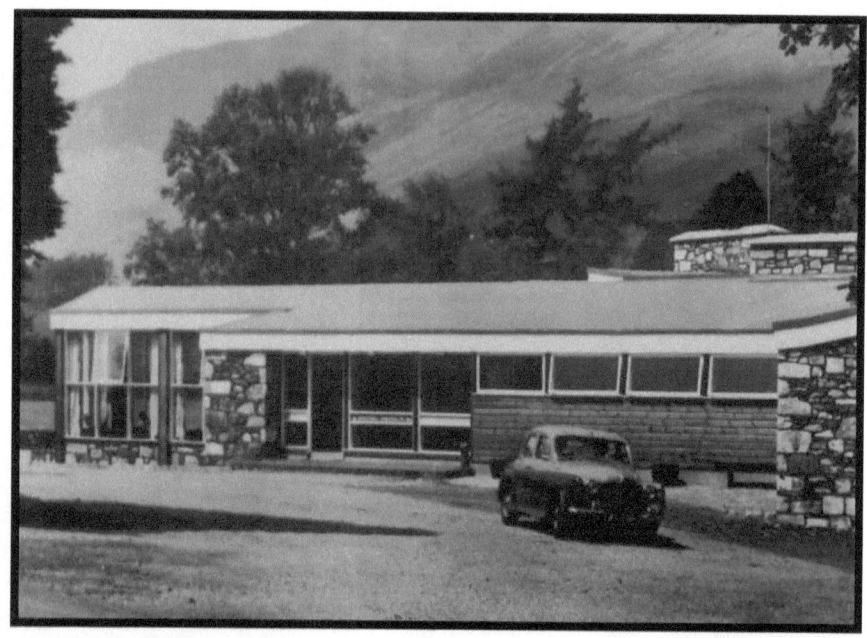

The Scandinavian-style façade of the new hotel (above) and the lounge (below), complete with deer antlers

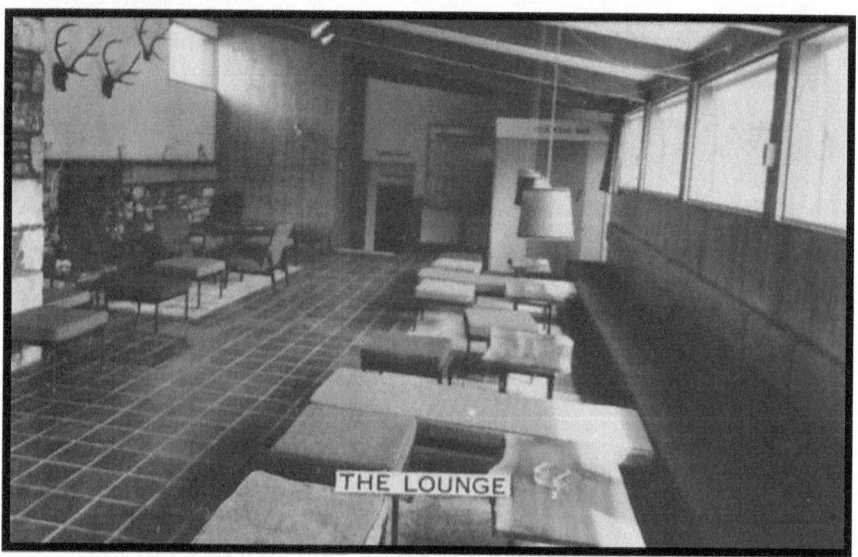

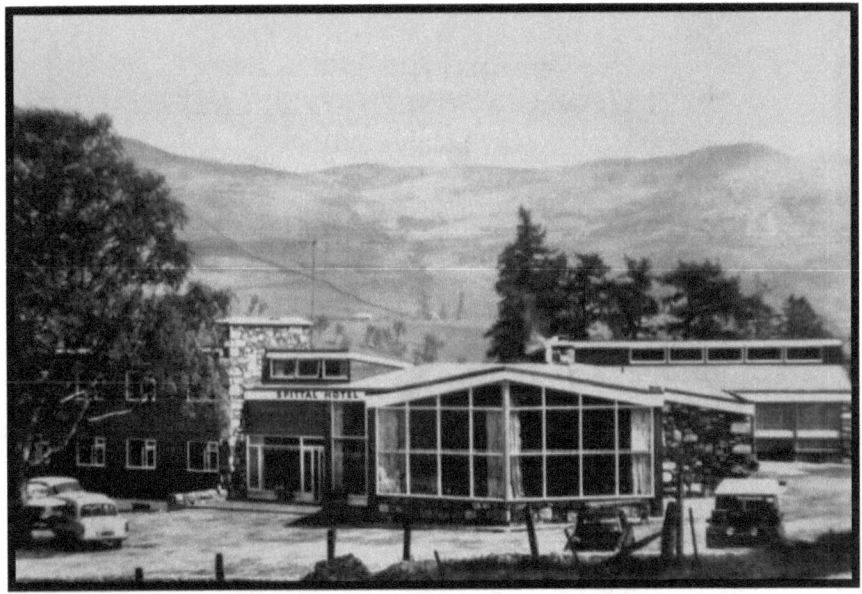

The main entrance of the Spittal Hotel (above) and the gable-end of a later extension (below)

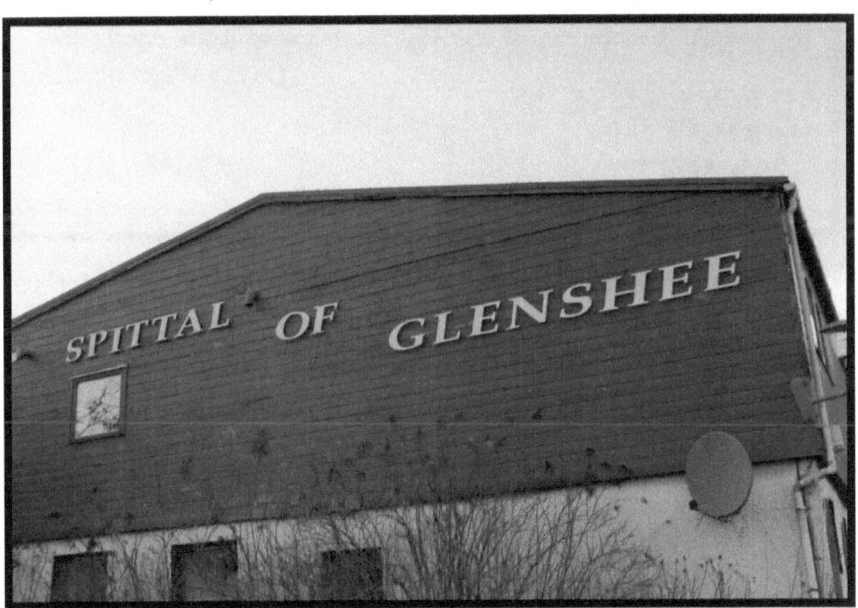

> The Companies Acts 1948 to 1967
> SPITTAL OF GLENSHEE HOTEL, LIMITED
> (In Liquidation)
>
> AT an Extraordinary General Meeting of the Members of the above named Company held at the Spittal of Glenshee Hotel Limited, Glenshee, by Blairgowrie, Perthshire, on 28th April 1980, the following Special Resolution was duly passed:—
>
> "That the Company be forthwith wound up voluntarily and that DAVID WATSON, Chartered Accountant, 147 Bath Street, Glasgow G2 4SN, be and is hereby appointed Liquidator for the purposes of such winding up."
>
> ROBERT E. PARKIN, Chairman.
>
> The Companies Acts 1948 to 1967
> SPITTAL OF GLENSHEE HOTEL LIMITED
> Members' Voluntary Winding Up
>
> I, DAVID WATSON, Chartered Accountant, 147 Bath Street, Glasgow, hereby give notice that I have been appointed Liquidator of the SPITTAL OF GLENSHEE HOTEL LIMITED by Special Resolution of the Company dated 28th April 1980.
>
> DAVID WATSON, C.A.
>
> 147 Bath Street,
> Glasgow G2 4SN.
> 28th April 1980.

While the 1970s and 80s were among the best years for skiing in Glenshee, the Spittal of Glenshee Hotel did not fare quite so well and, in 1980, the company went into liquidation and the business was wound up. However, the hotel continued to trade under new owners.

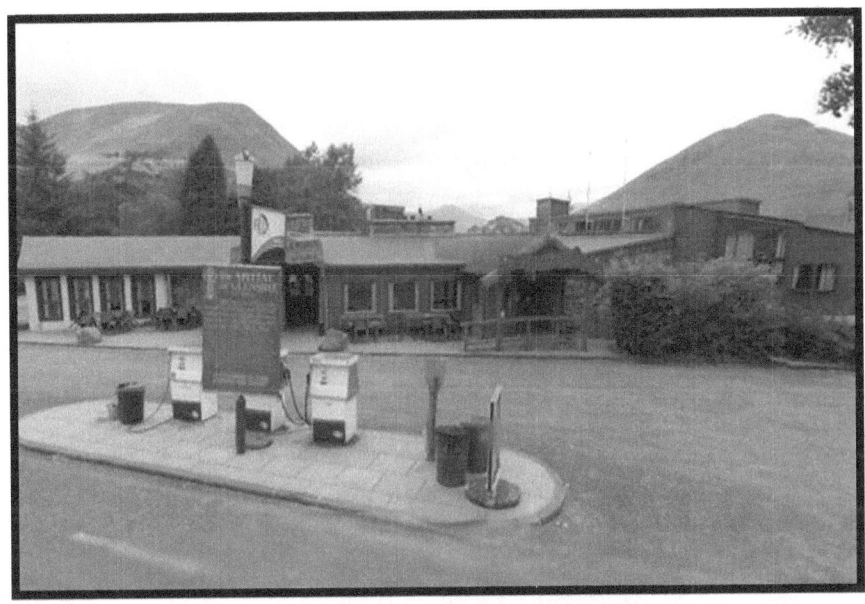

In later years, the hotel was the only place to buy fuel on the road between Blairgowrie and Braemar

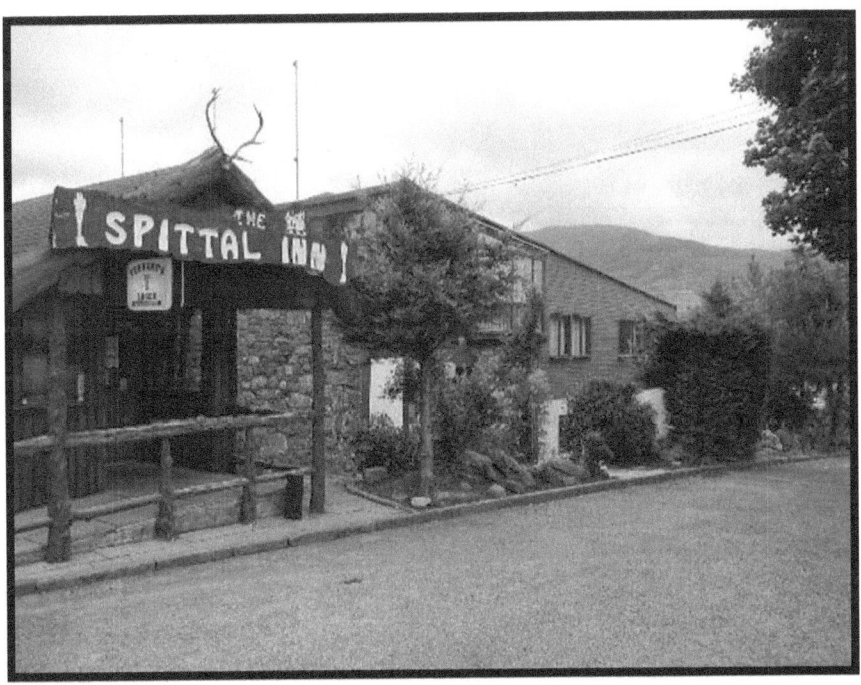

Over the years the hotel has been adapted and extended to meet the needs of both guests and its various owners.

The most significant development was the addition of a two-storey wing at the back of the site which increased the number of bedrooms to 54.

In 1987 owners Huntingtower Hotels Company Ltd received planning permission for extensions and alterations at the property.

Six years later, in 1993, plans to alter and extend the hotel and erect a heritage centre on the site were also approved.

Plans for new signage and flagpoles lodged in the same year were rejected, despite the work having been undertaken, while, in 2004 building warrants were granted for the installation of en-suite facilities in the bedrooms.

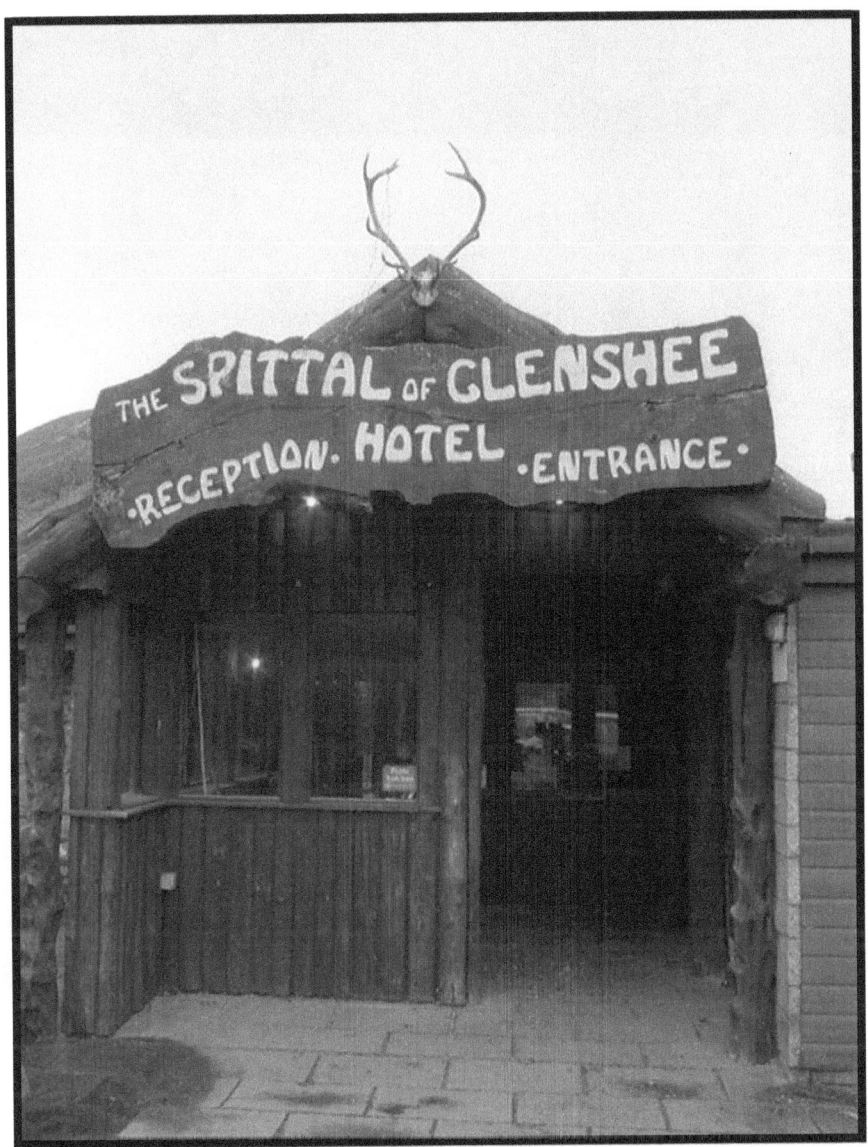

The entrance as it was in later years

'Perfectly adequate facilities, good location and reasonable price. Staff excellent - friendly and efficient.'

Guest review, April 2009

The accommodation was clean, comfortable and economical. The breakfast was of a good quality and we would both return there and be prepared to recommend to others.'

Guest review, September 2011

'I have been before and just love the place. Going again soon.'

Guest review, November 2012

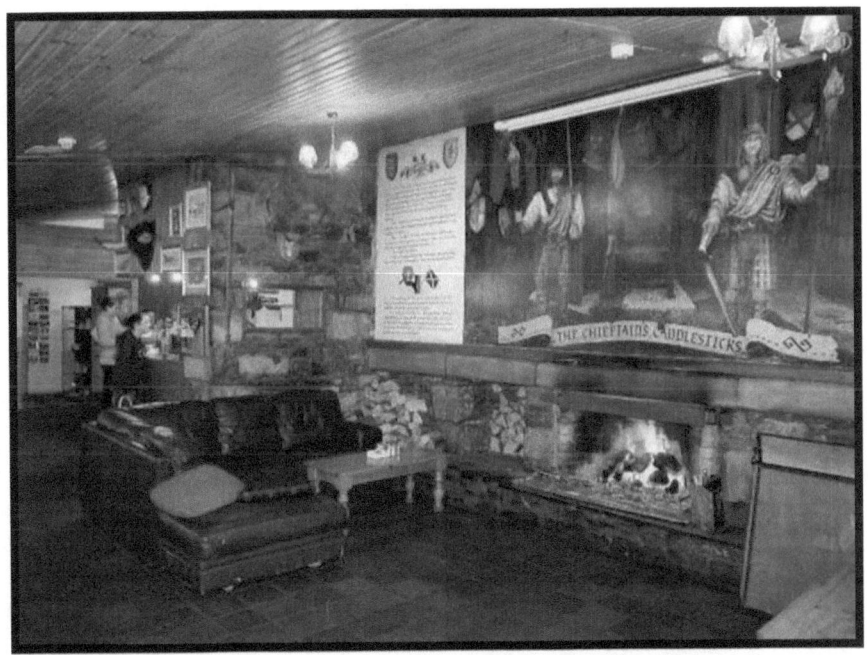

A mural extolling the hotel's Highland heritage (above) was painted over the fireplace in the bar (below)

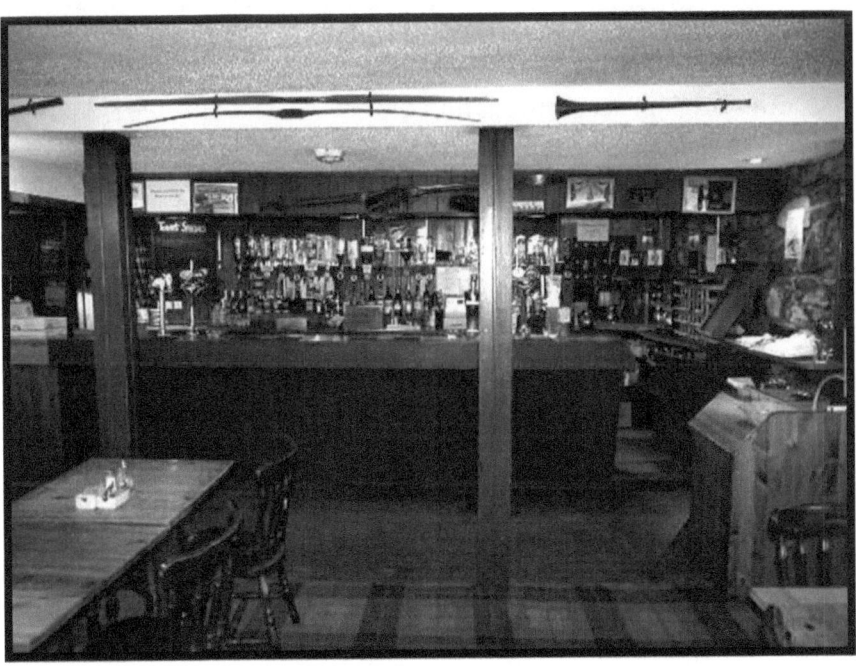

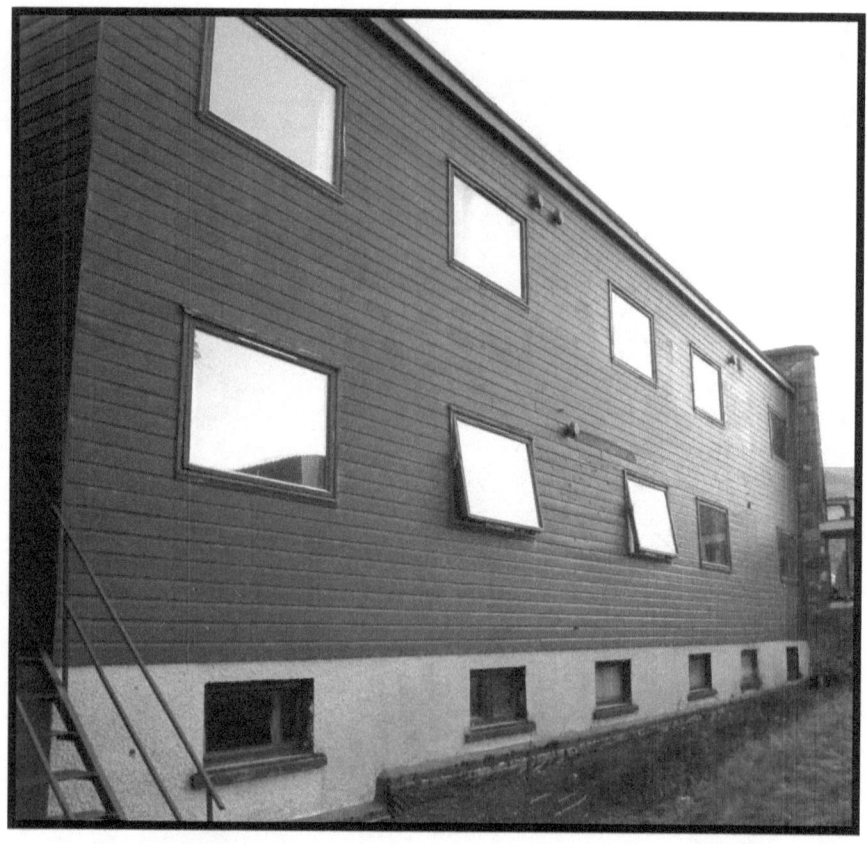

The original accommodation block

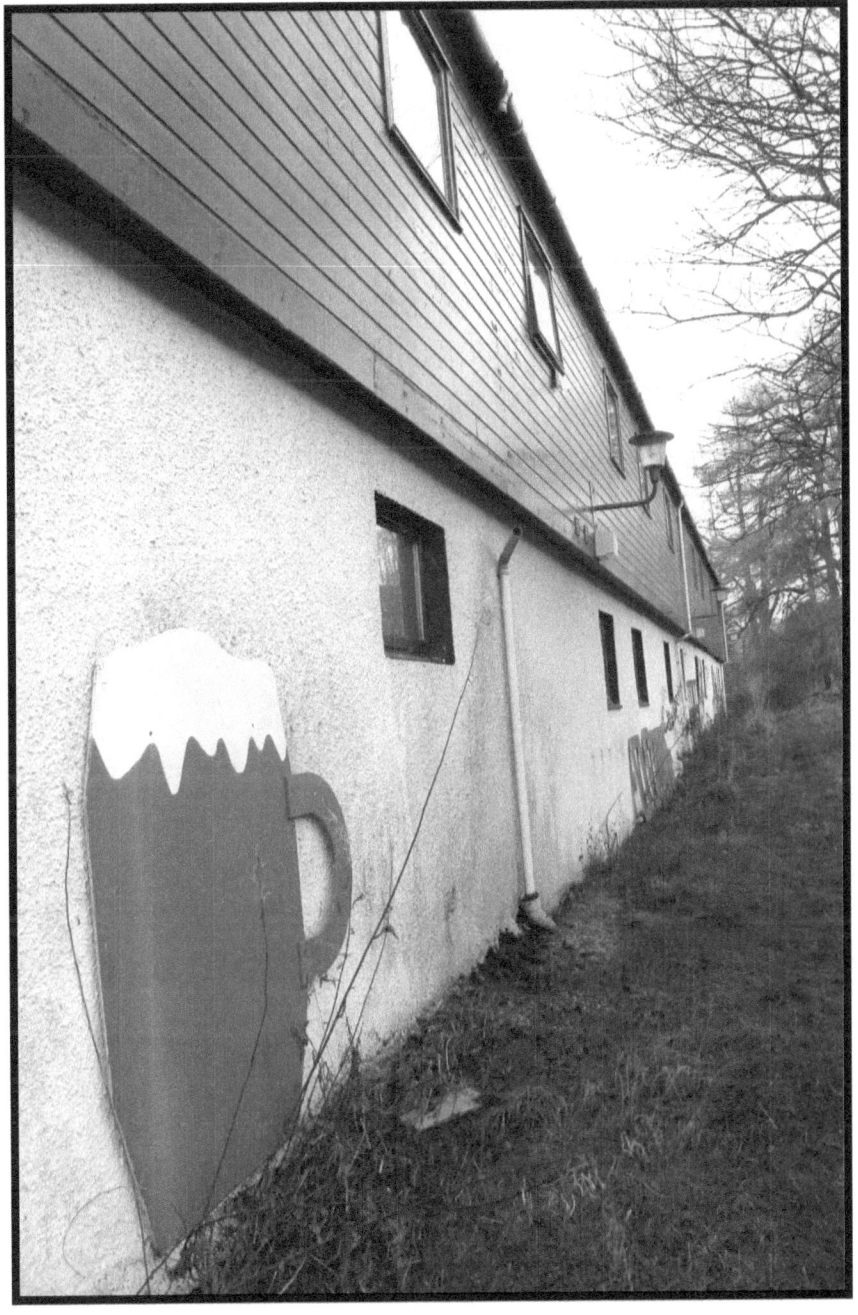

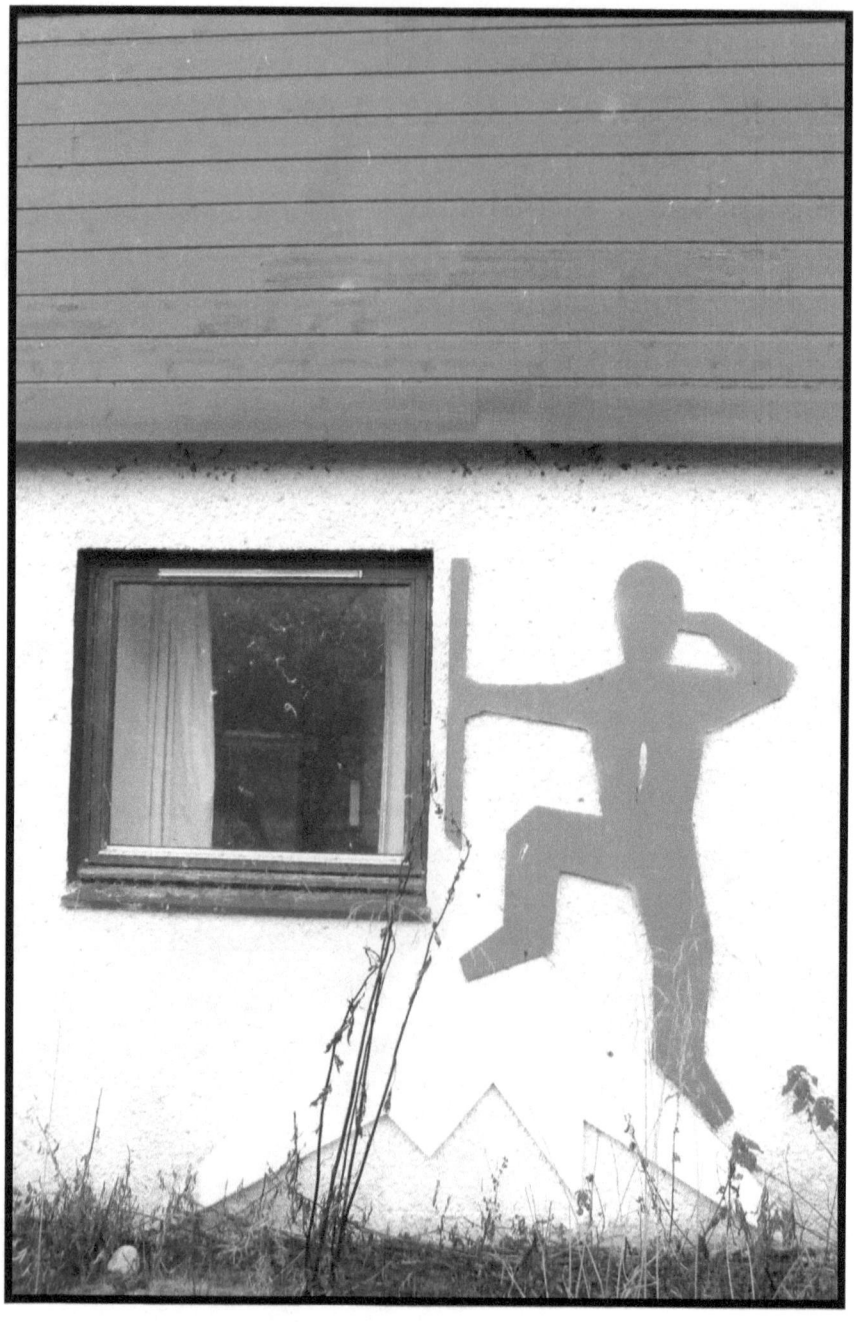

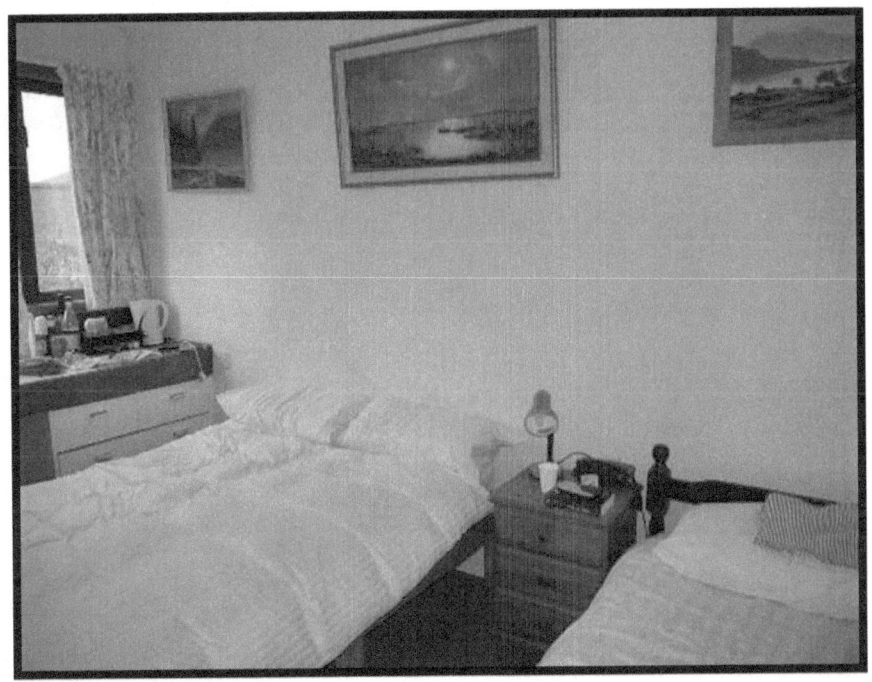

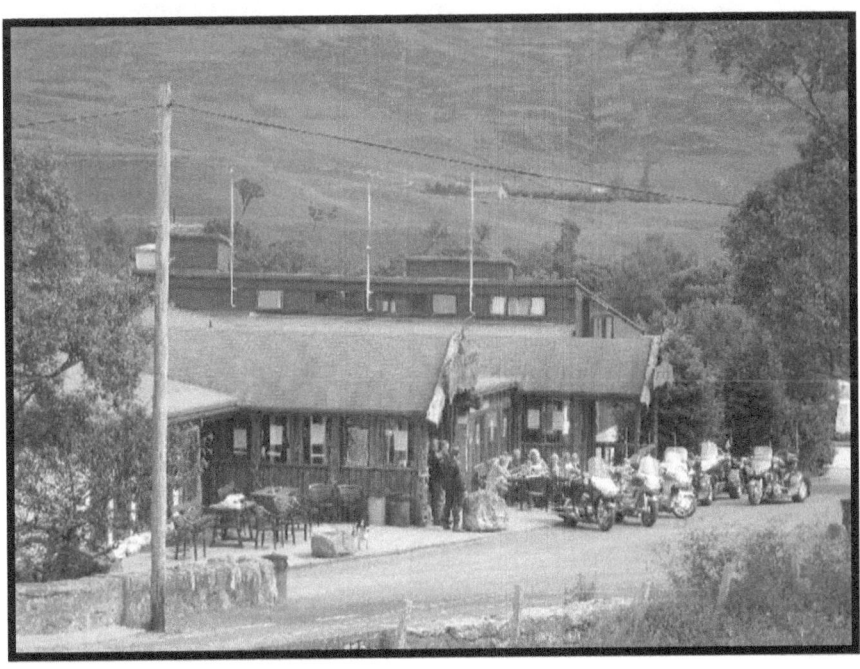

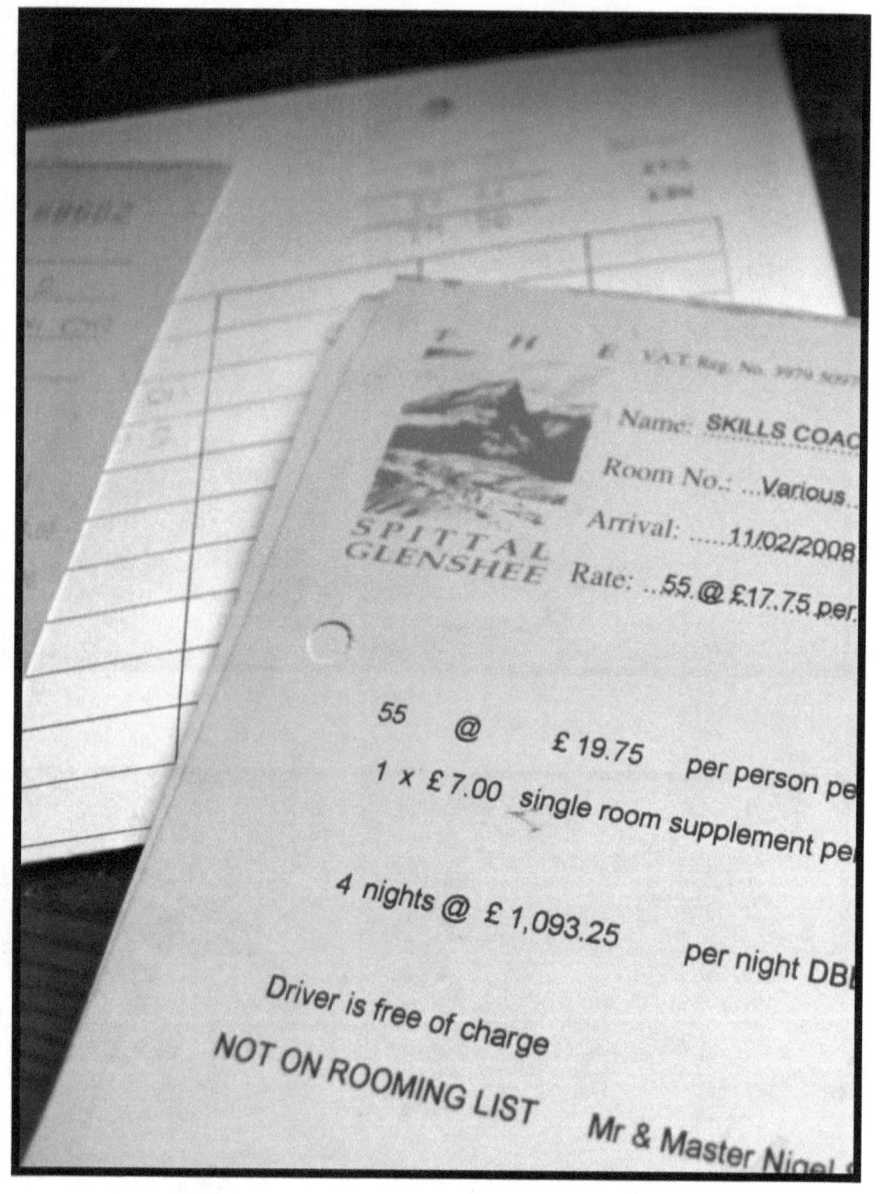

The Scottish ski industry has always been at the mercy of the weather and, following a succession of poor winter seasons, the Glenshee Chairlift Company Ltd was forced into receivership in 2004. However, a management buyout ensured ski-ing continued, although a growing trend towards skiers visiting the glen for the day, rather than staying overnight, developed.

Some hostelries on the ski road north from Blairgowrie shut down – the Dalrulzion Hotel and Blackwater Inn along them – while the Spittal of Glenshee Hotel became increasingly reliant on the lower end of the coach party market to fill its rooms. Efforts to bolster income included the opening of a bunkhouse and campsite on the grounds.

In 2008, tour groups were enjoying rates as low as £17.75 a head for dinner, bed and breakfast while individual guests could book in from as little as £20 a night bed and breakfast.

While the hotel continued to enjoy positive feedback from guests until 2013, a spate of unfavourable reviews the following year suggested all was not well.

'A very run-down hotel.'

Guest review, December 2013

'I have been to this cafe/bar/restaurant many times in years past and it has been a lovely, fun stop following winter sports on the slopes, with the roaring fire to cosy in front of, great banter at the bar, parlour games being played and lots of good food and home bakes. I don't know what has happened to the place... a landslide downhill!'

Guest review, January 2014

'Hotel feels damp and old. Although it had character and a certain charm I can't help feeling a small face lift is required. The manager seemed to be missing and no one was able to say when they were likely to return. Have not been seen for two weeks. The lack of management was evident.'

Guest review, March 2014

'I want to like this place but it's obviously going off the rails. When I first came here five or six years ago it was rather unique and well kept. Now it looks dilapidated and close to closure.'

Guest review, April 2014

'Sadly we arrived to an untidy hotel and one with too few staff to make it the destination it should really be.'

Guest review, June 2014

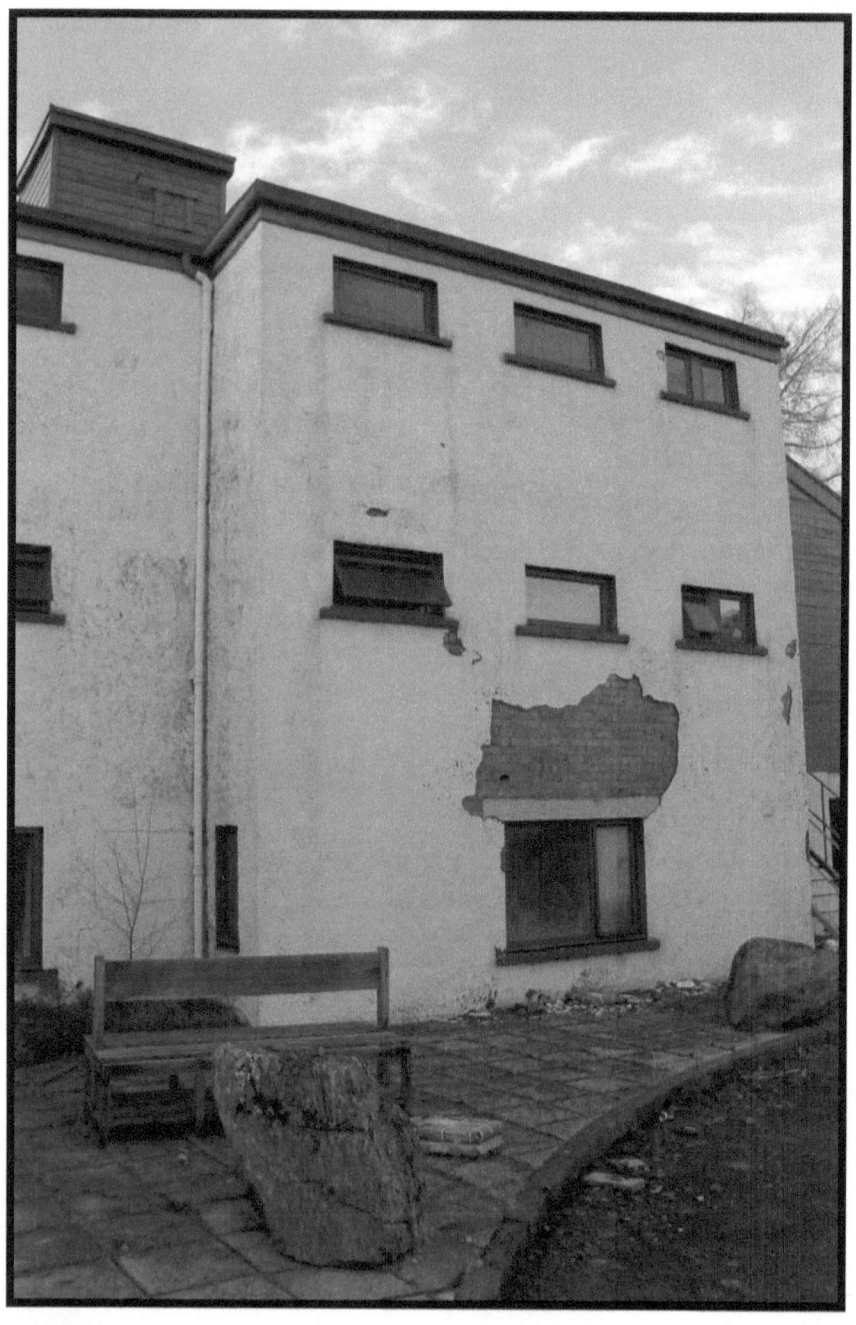

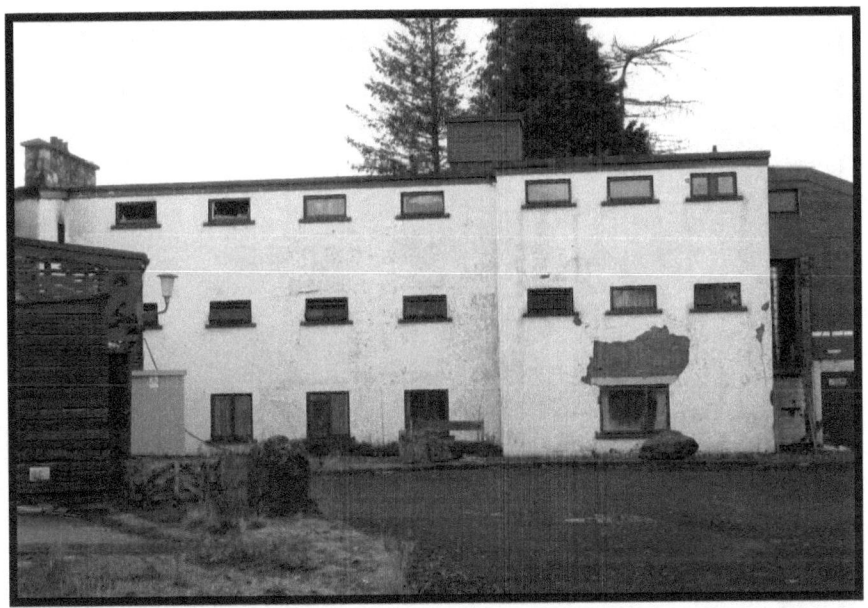

The hotel closed its doors to customers for the last time in June 2014, ostensibly for refurbishment amid rumours the business had either been put up for sale or sold.

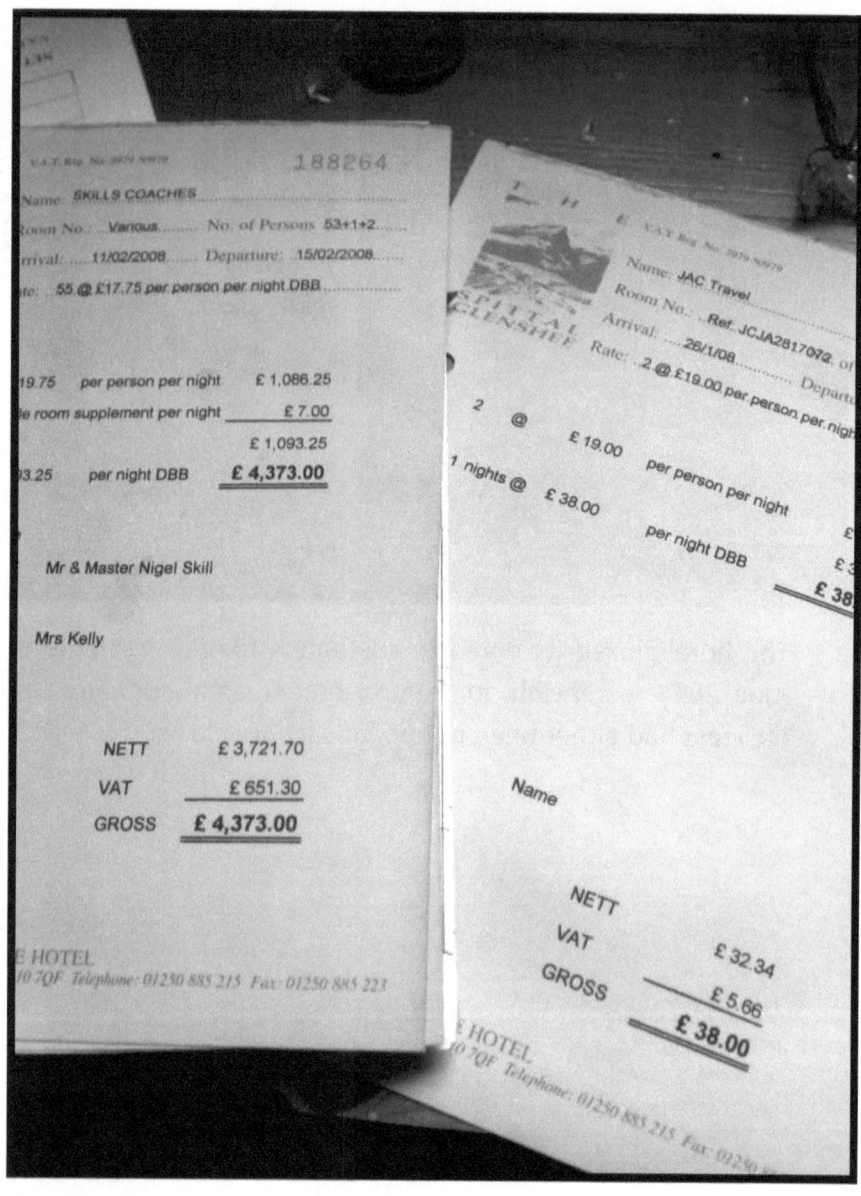

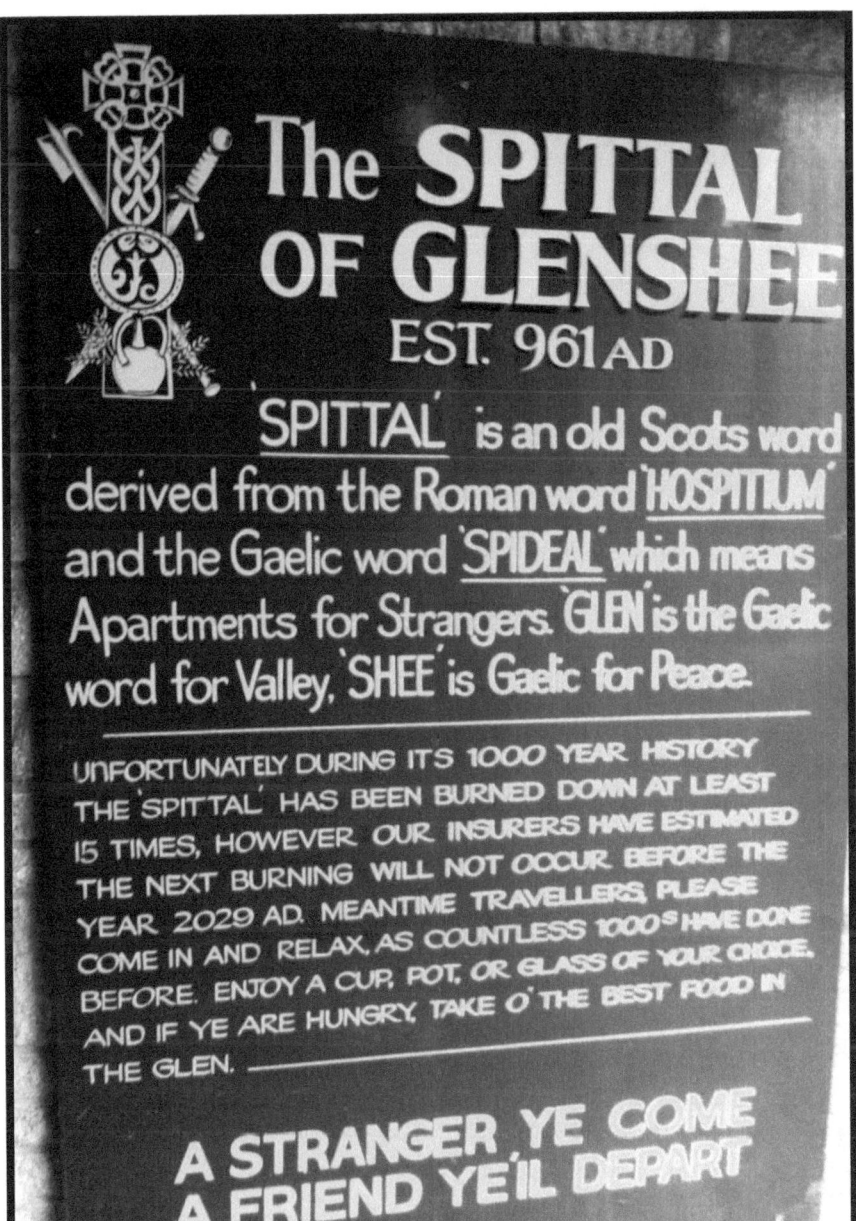

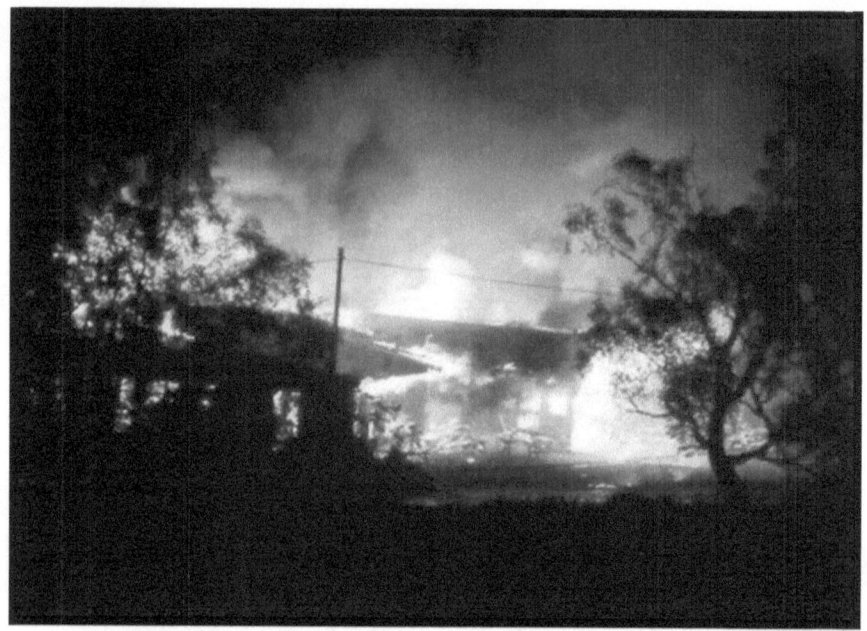

Ironically, the proprietors predicted, on a board welcoming visitors to the premises, that the hotel would, once again, burn down. Unfortunately, their estimate of this not happening before 2029 was wide of the mark.

During the early hours of Monday, August 18, 2014, fire broke out. Despite the best efforts of firefighters, by daybreak, a significant portion of the complex had been completely destroyed.

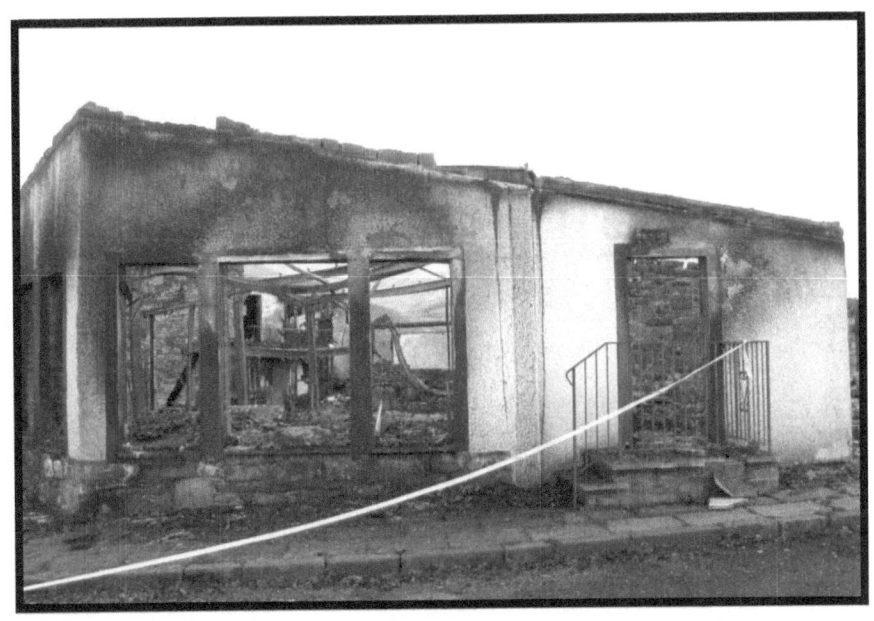

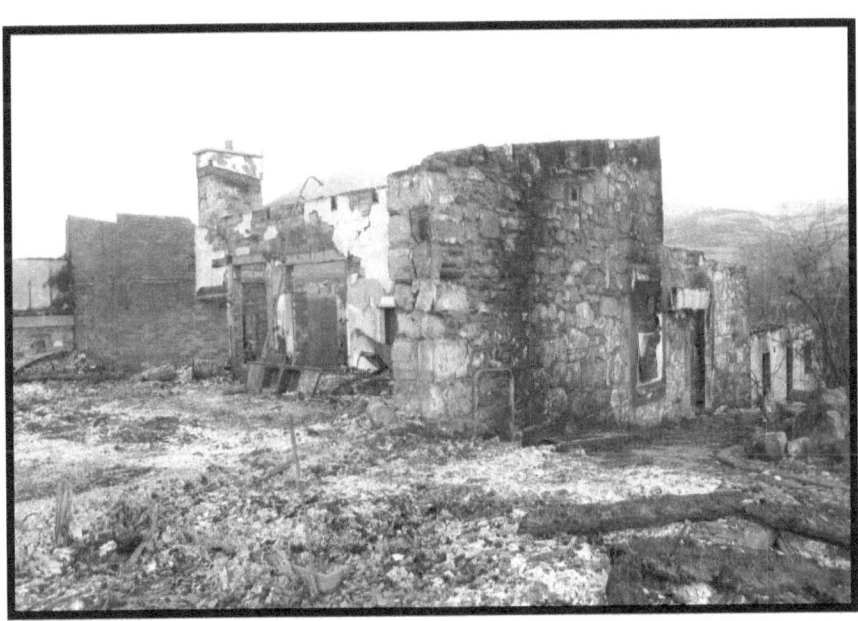

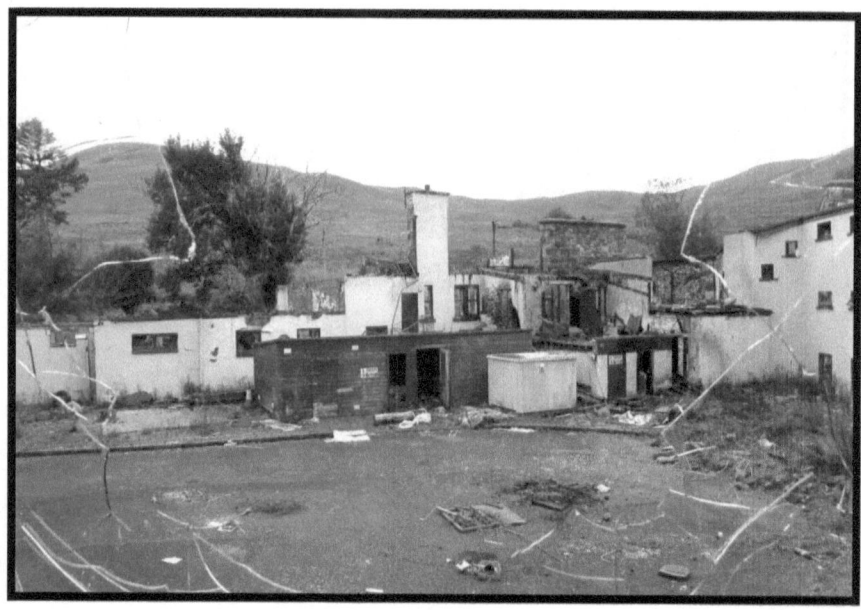

The fire ravaged the front third of the hotel, the section of the building housing the reception, bar, restaurant, function suite, kitchen and stores. All were reduced to rubble. The adjoining three-storey accommodation block, consisting of two floors of guest bedrooms above a basement level of staff accommodation, suffered serious smoke damage on its upper levels, while the two-storey accommodation block at the back of the site escaped unscathed.

The hotel was empty at the time and there were no casualties. A subsequent investigation by police and the fire service was unable to pinpoint the exact cause of the fire but found no suspicious circumstances.

The site was subsequently put up for sale at offers over £250,000.

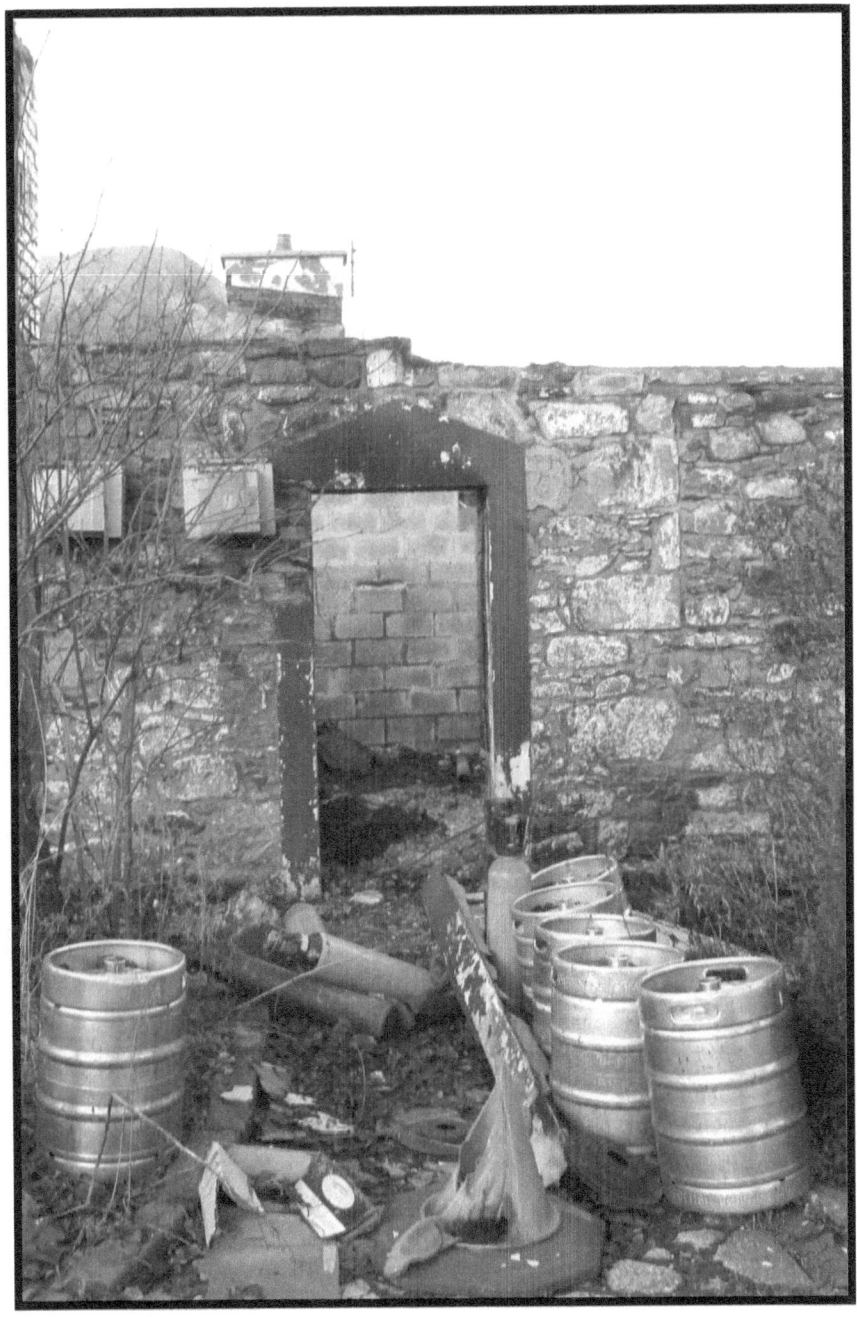

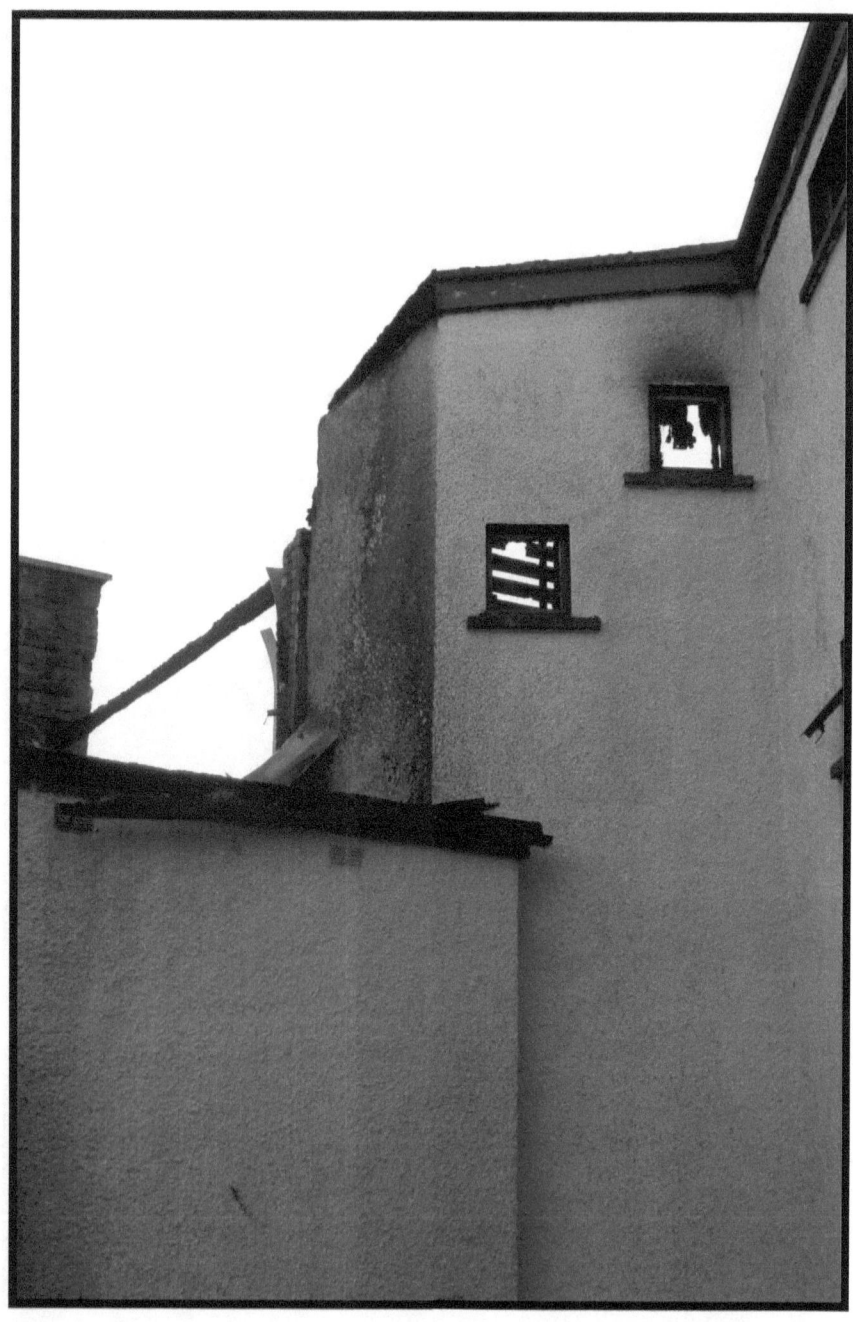

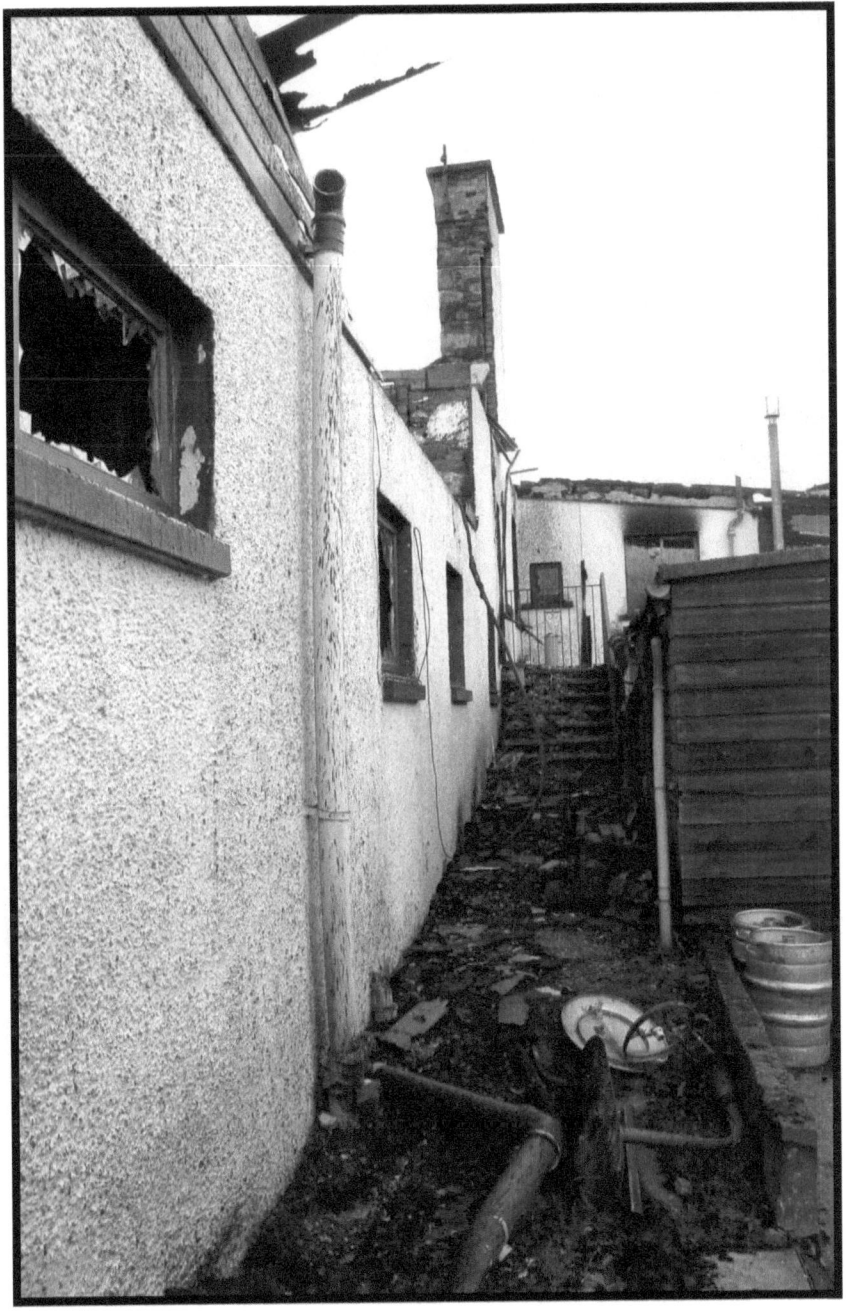

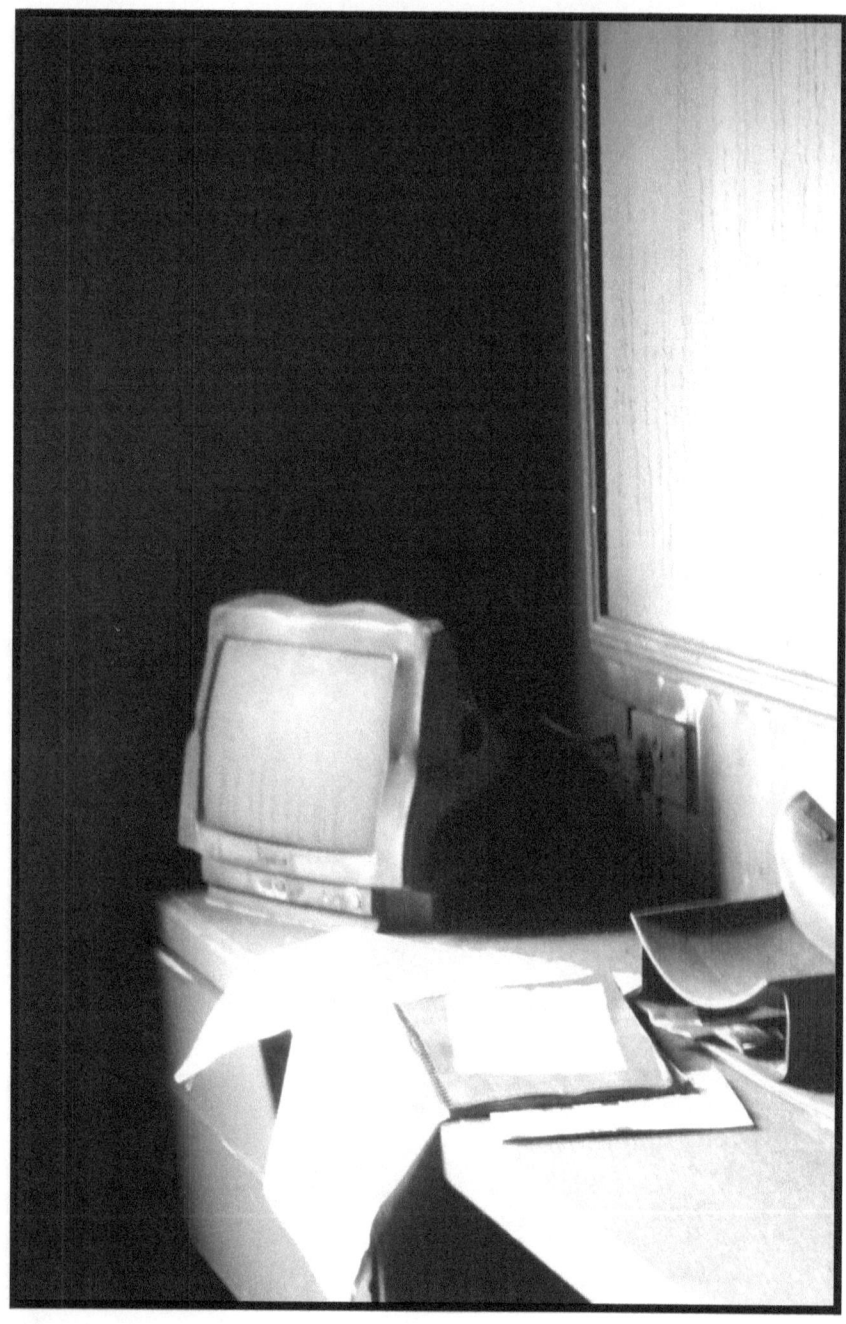

LIFE AND DEATH OF A HIGHLAND HOTEL

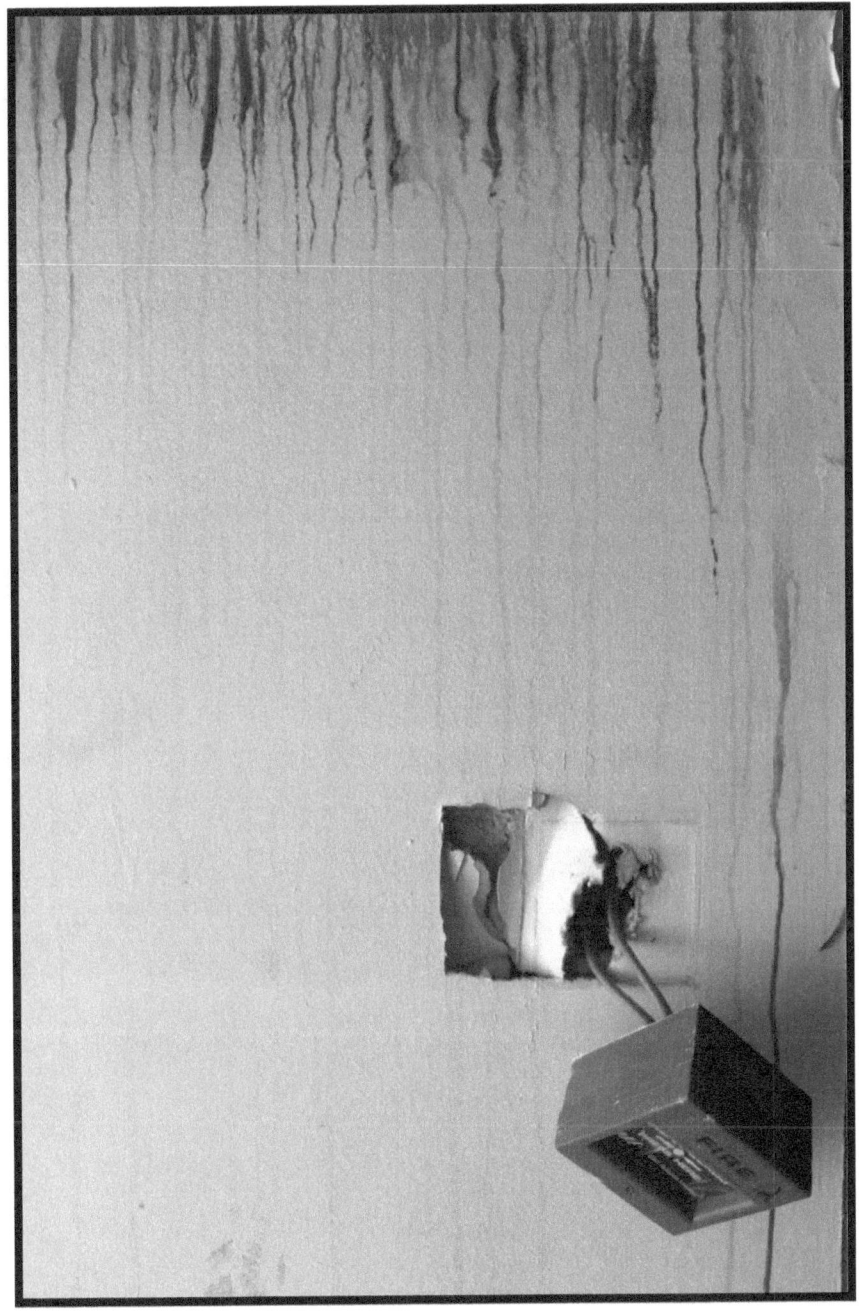

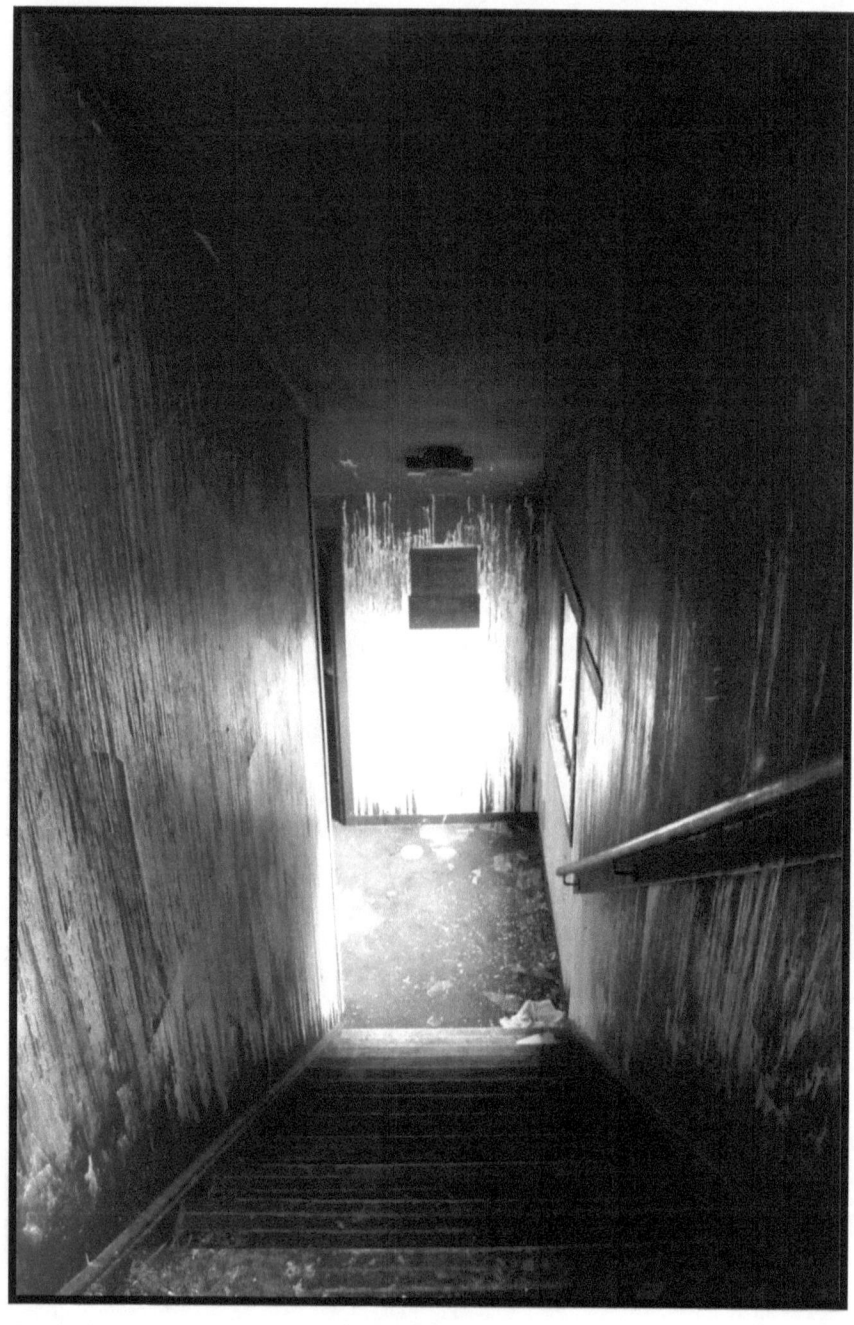

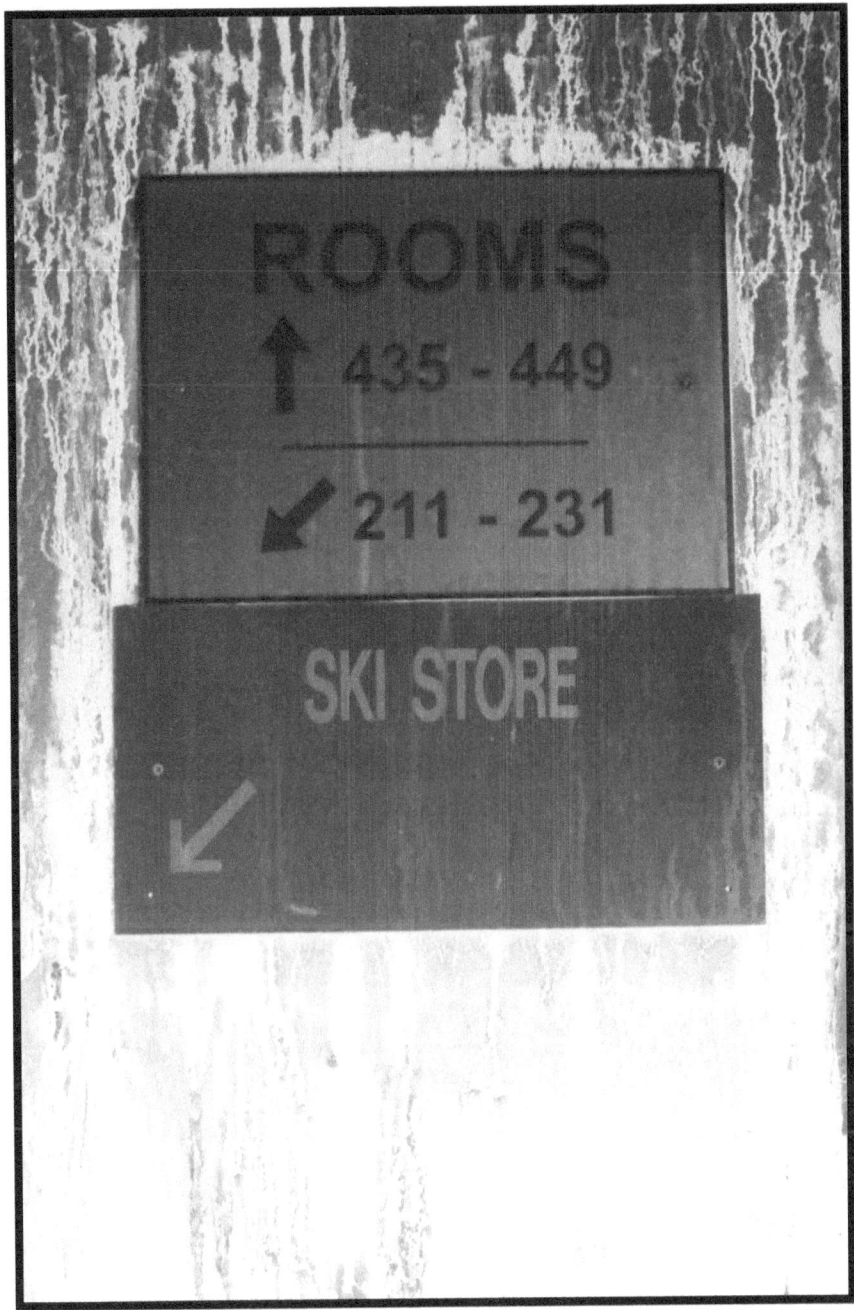

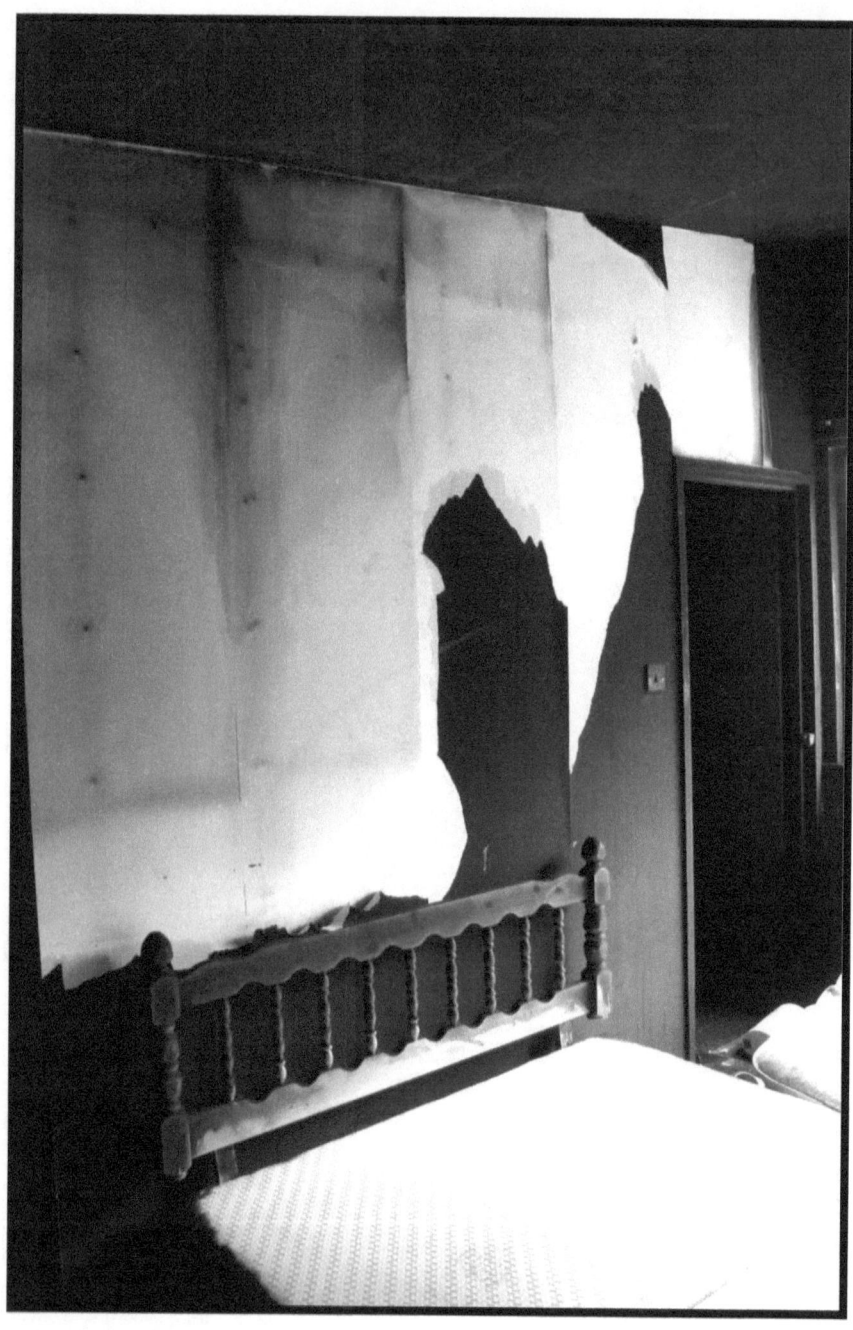

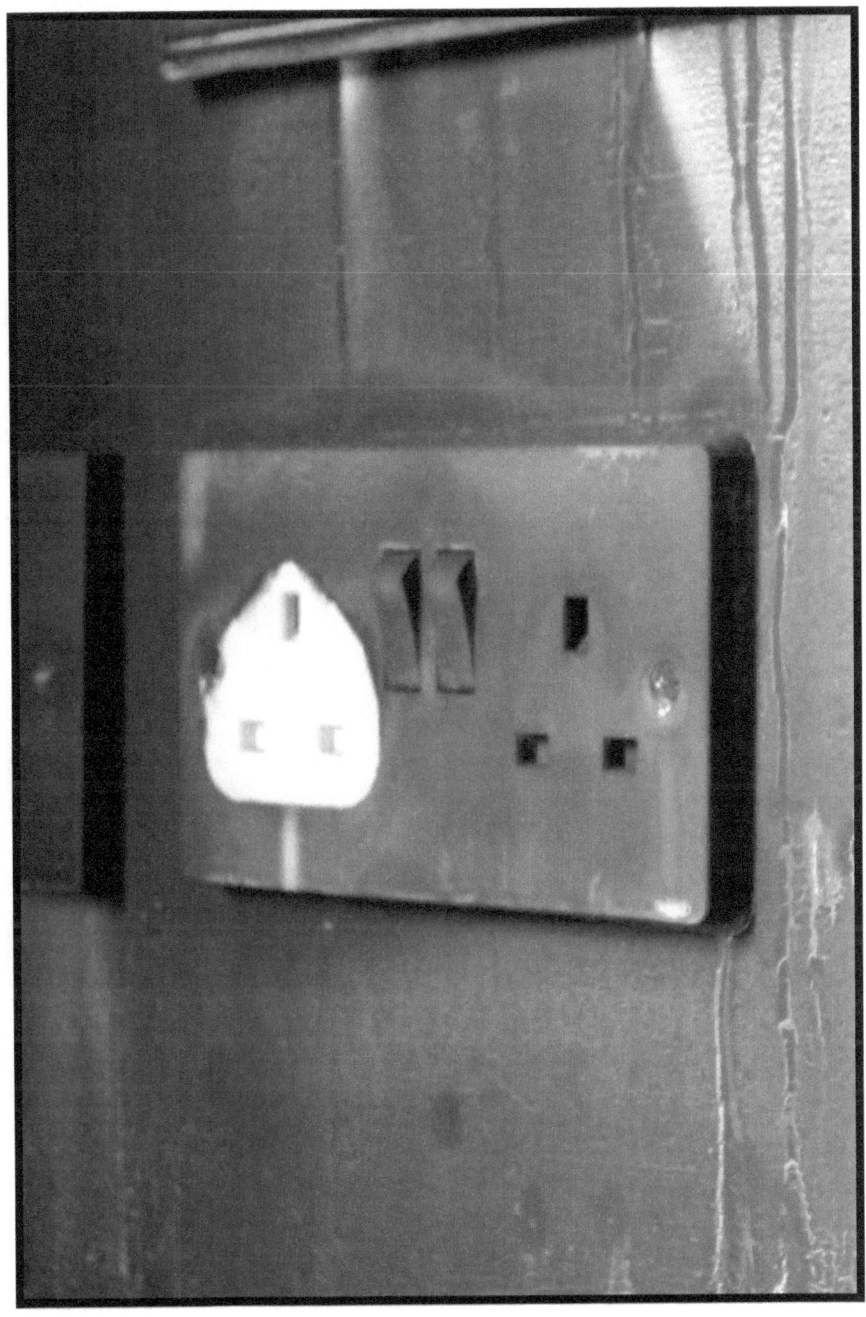

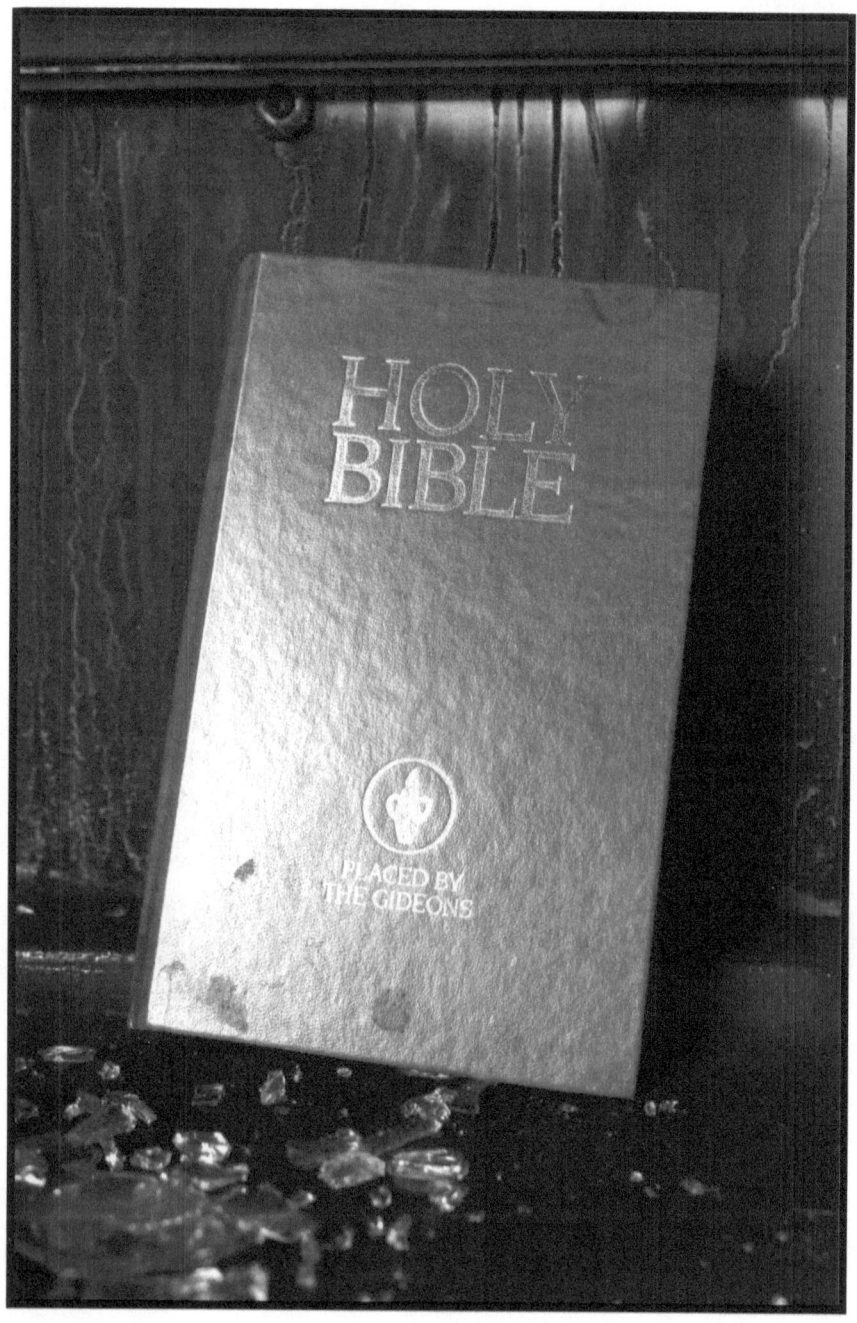

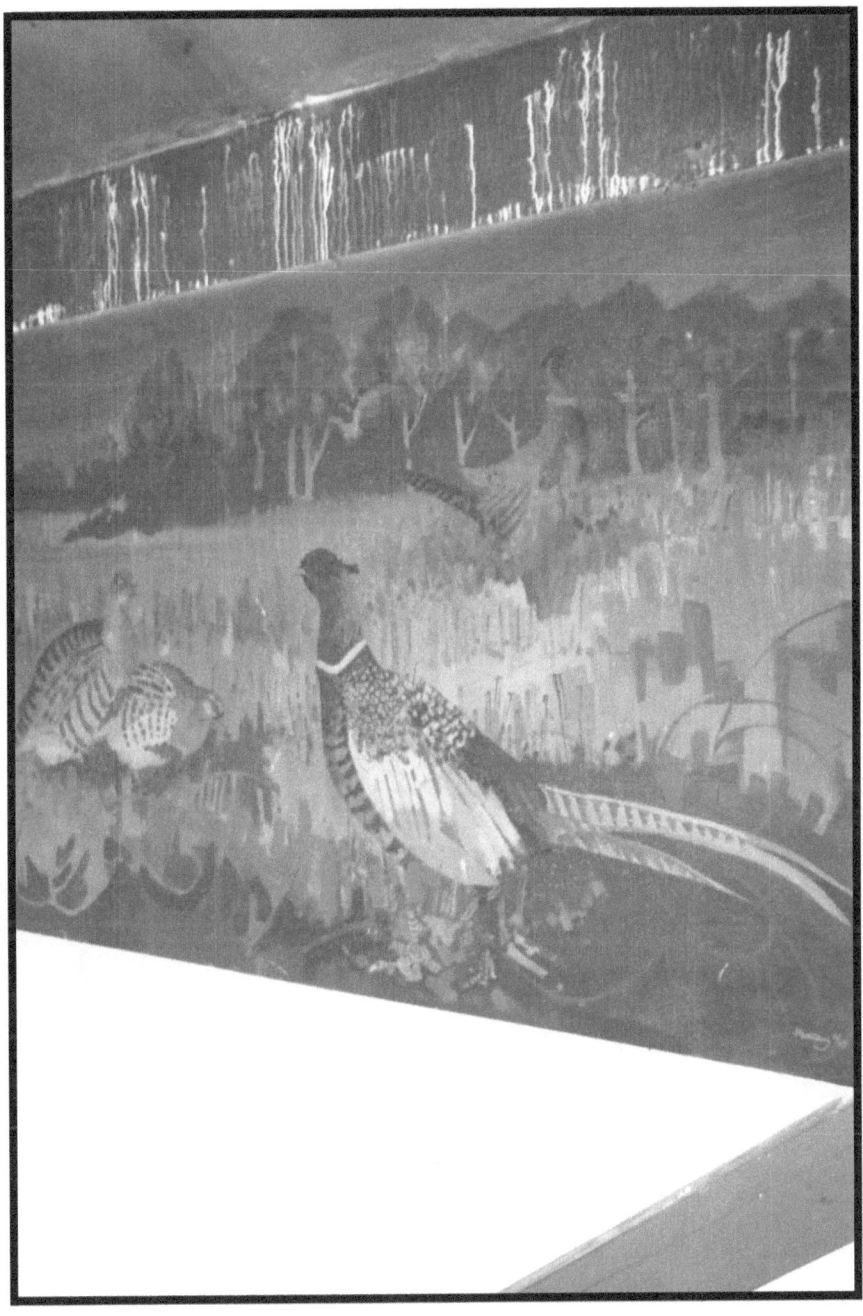

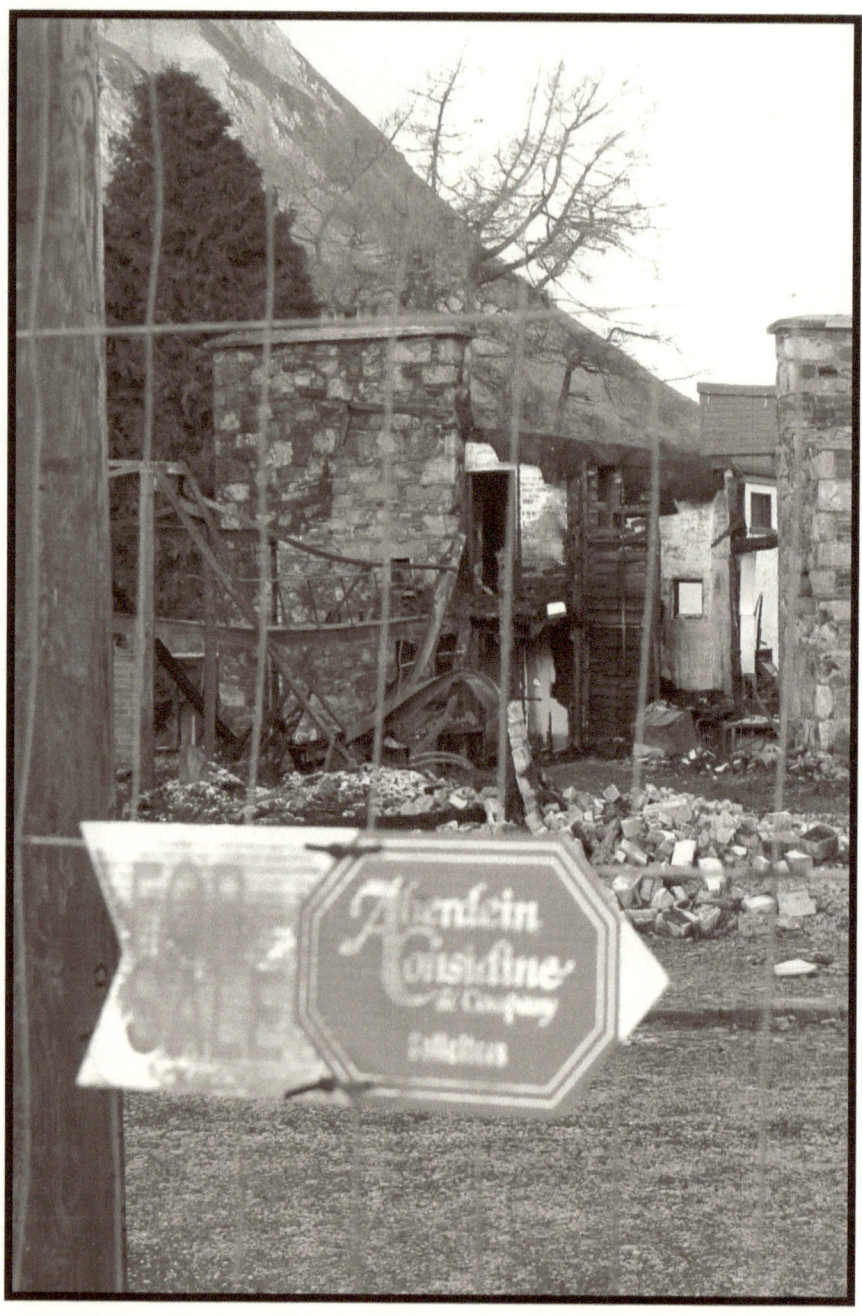

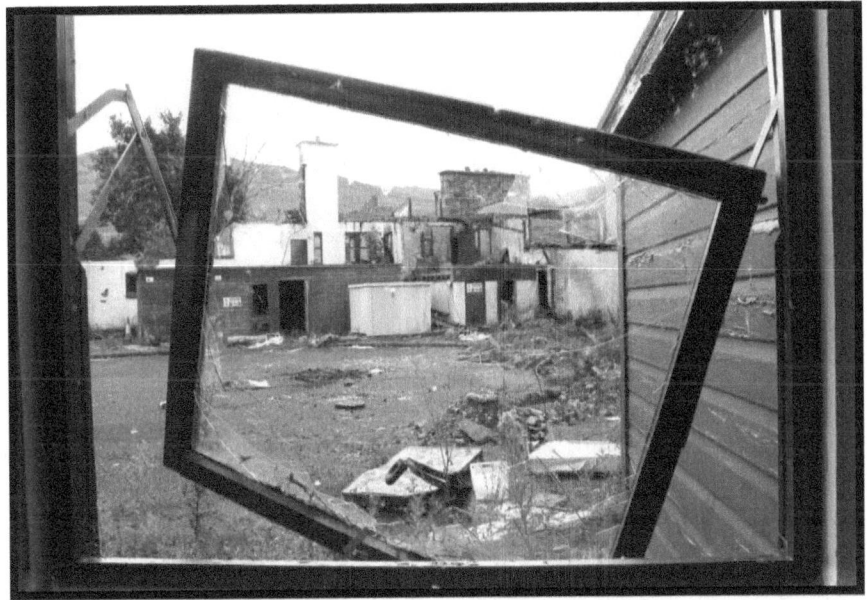

In September 2014, following the fire, owners Yorsipp Ltd, a Glasgow-based investment company, were given notice to secure the site and make the remaining structures safe.

Despite its remote rural location, the empty and abandoned hotel soon fell victim to vandalism. Doors were wrenched open and windows shattered. Toilets, showers and mirrors were smashed. Beds and furniture were upended and scattered across rooms. Holes were kicked in walls and cables hauled out.

In the end, after two centuries of service, the Spittal of Glenshee Hotel suffered a cruel and unceremonious demise.

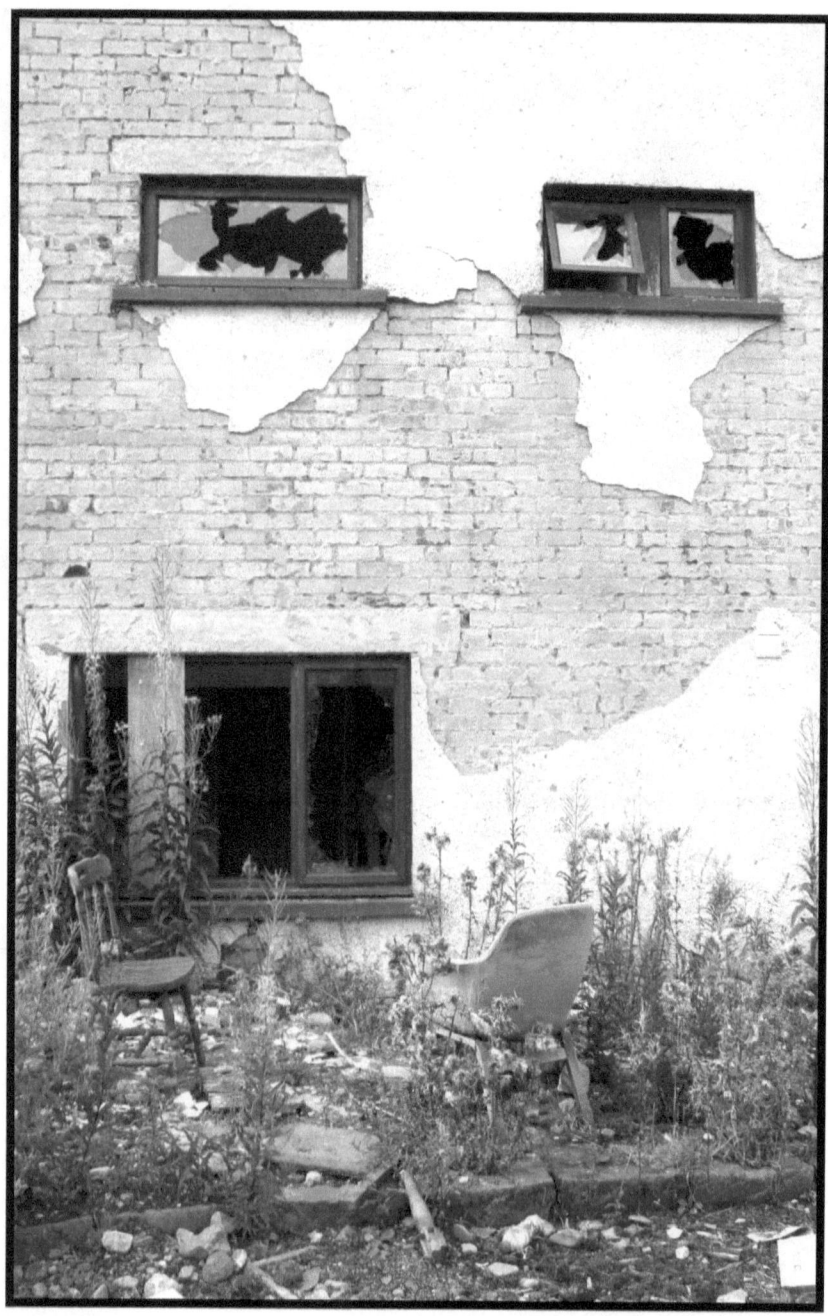

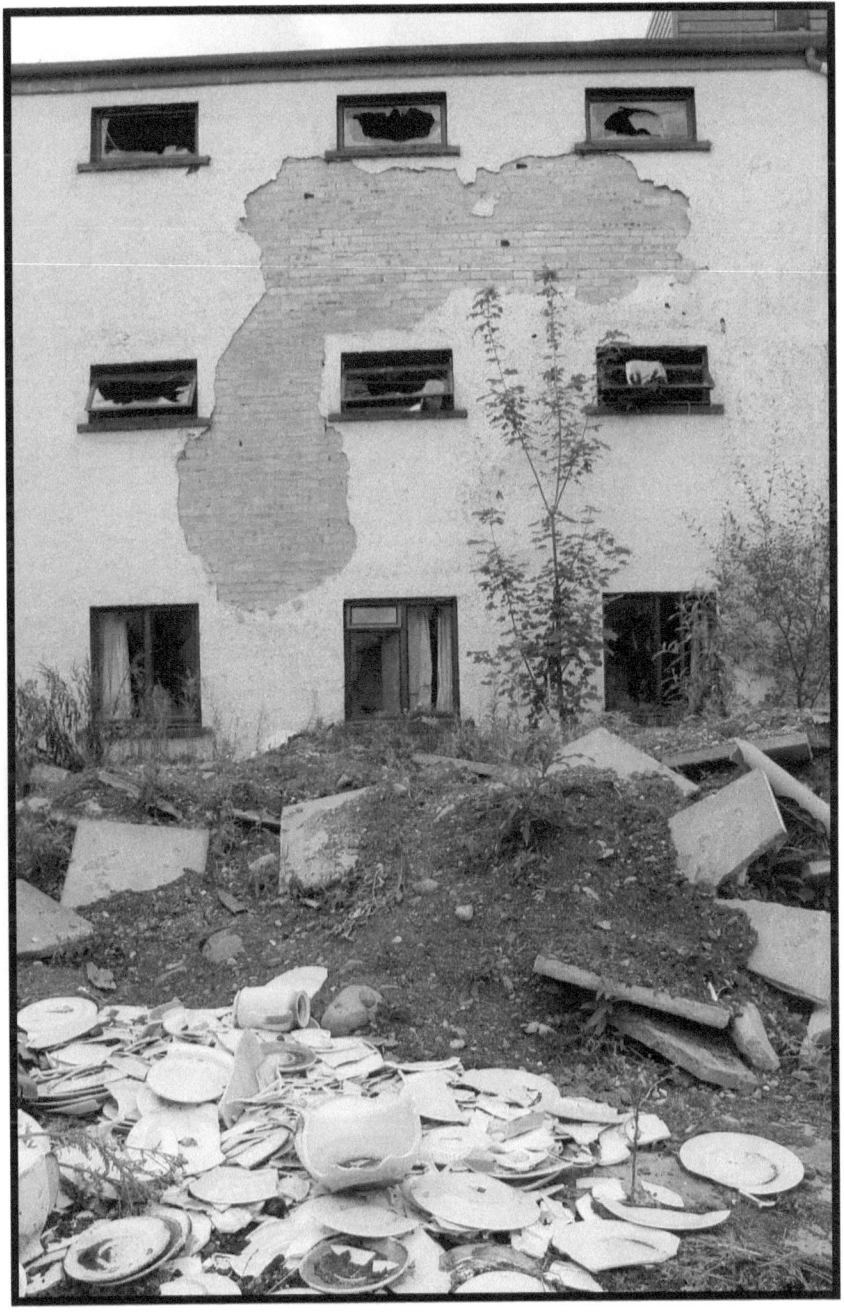

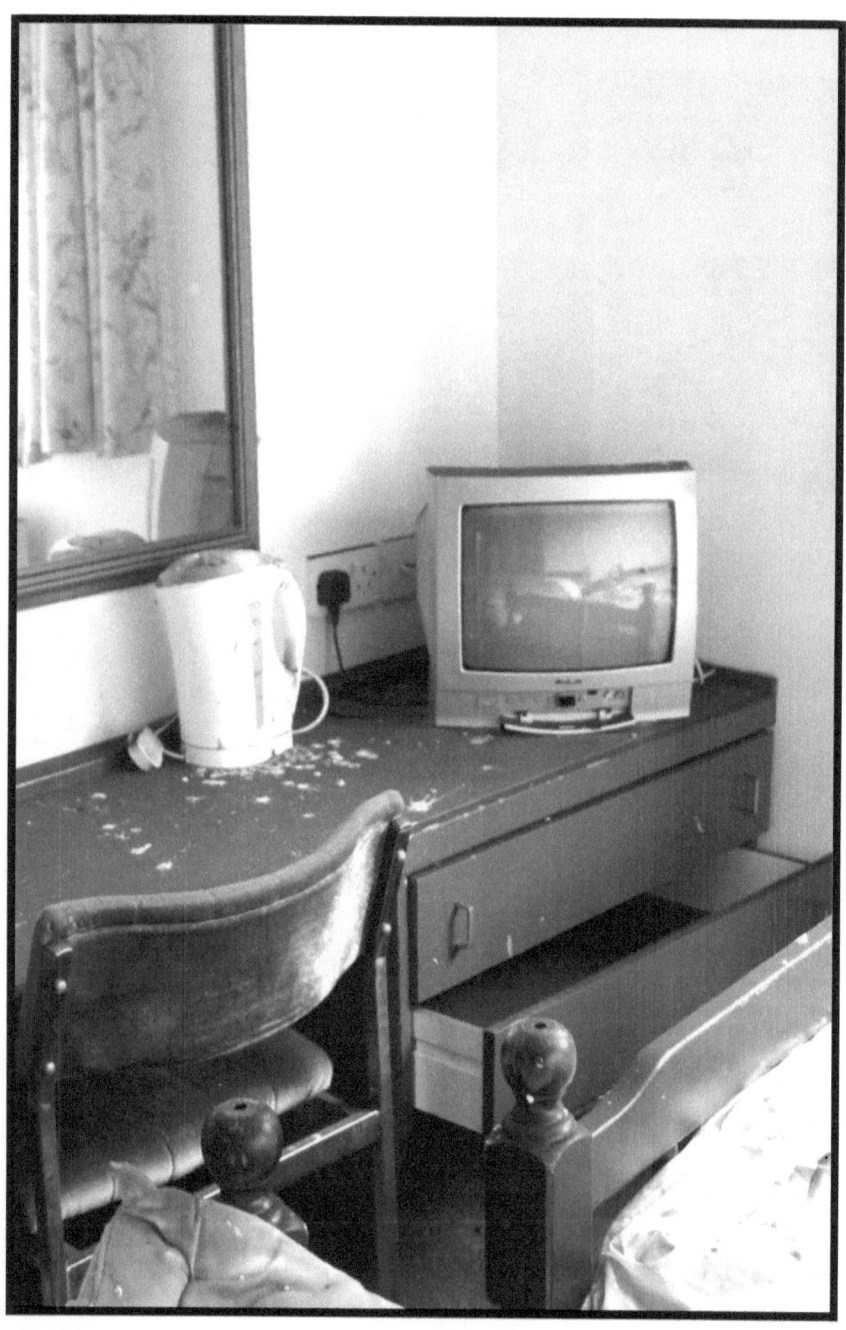

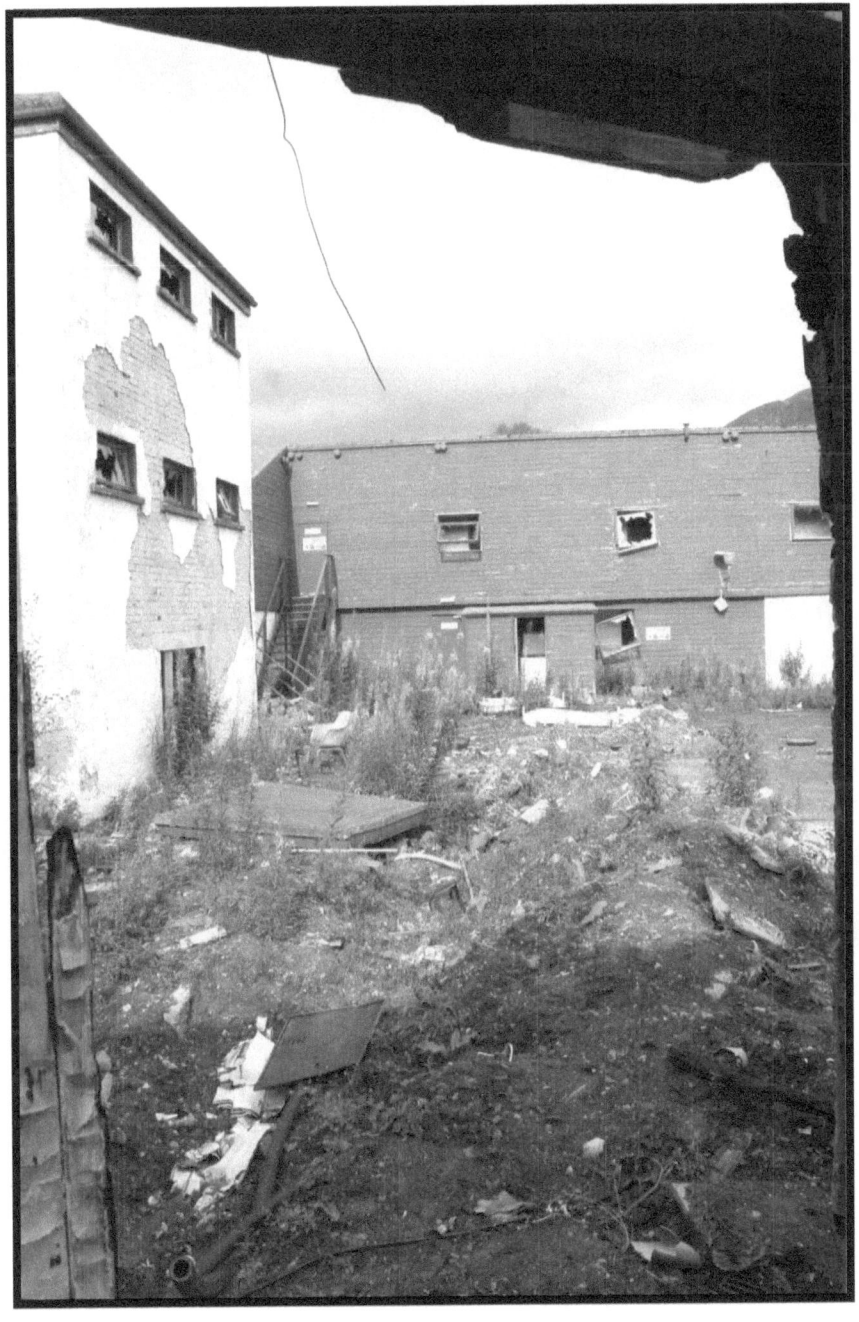

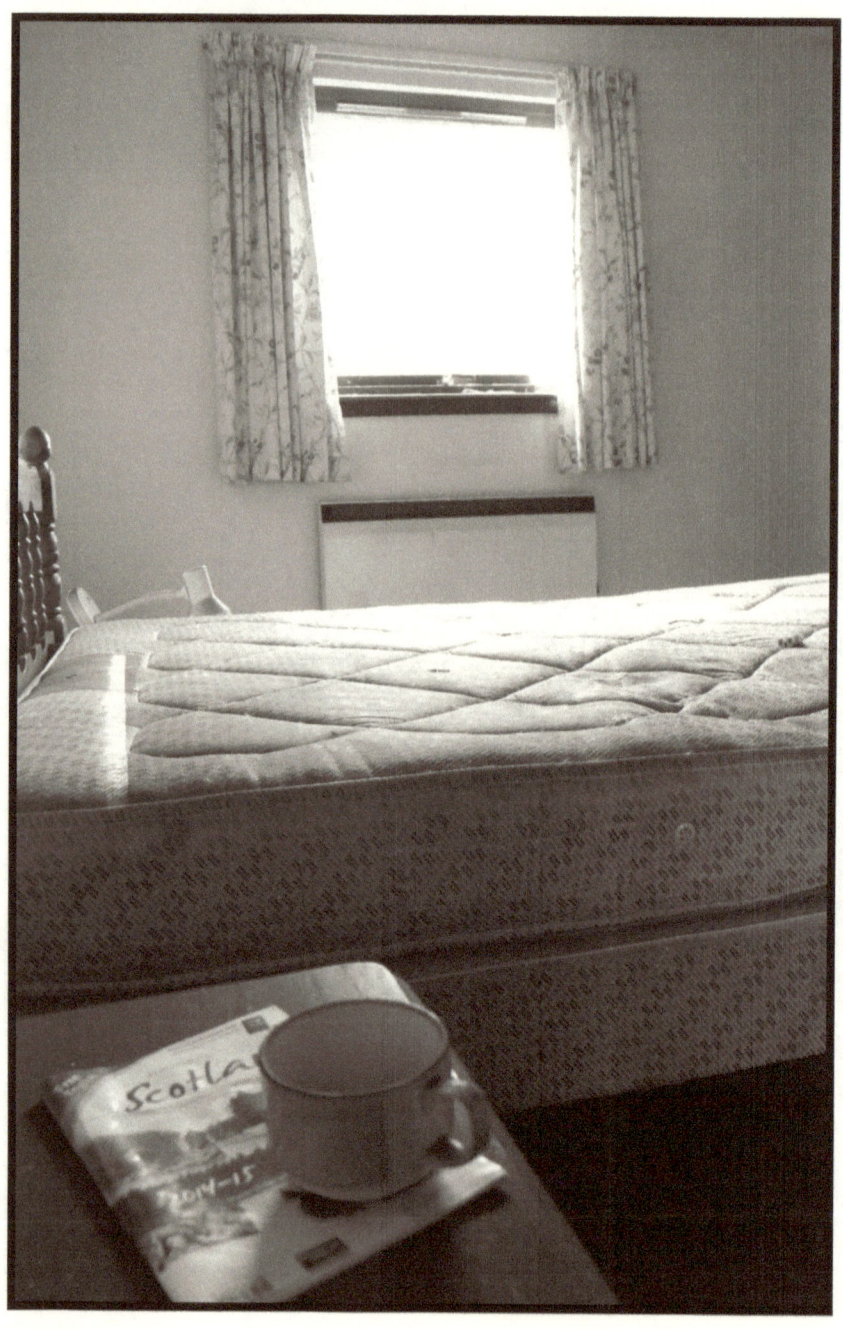

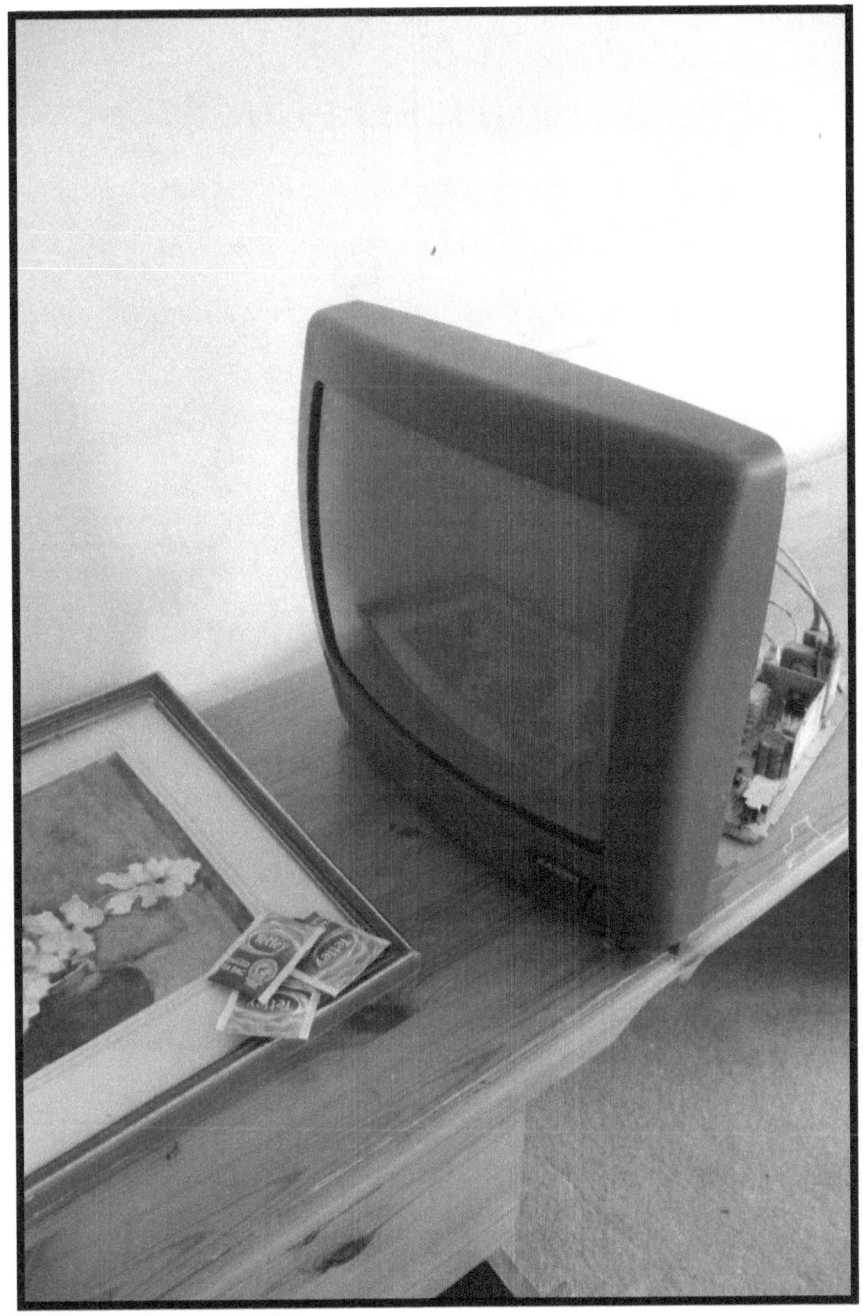

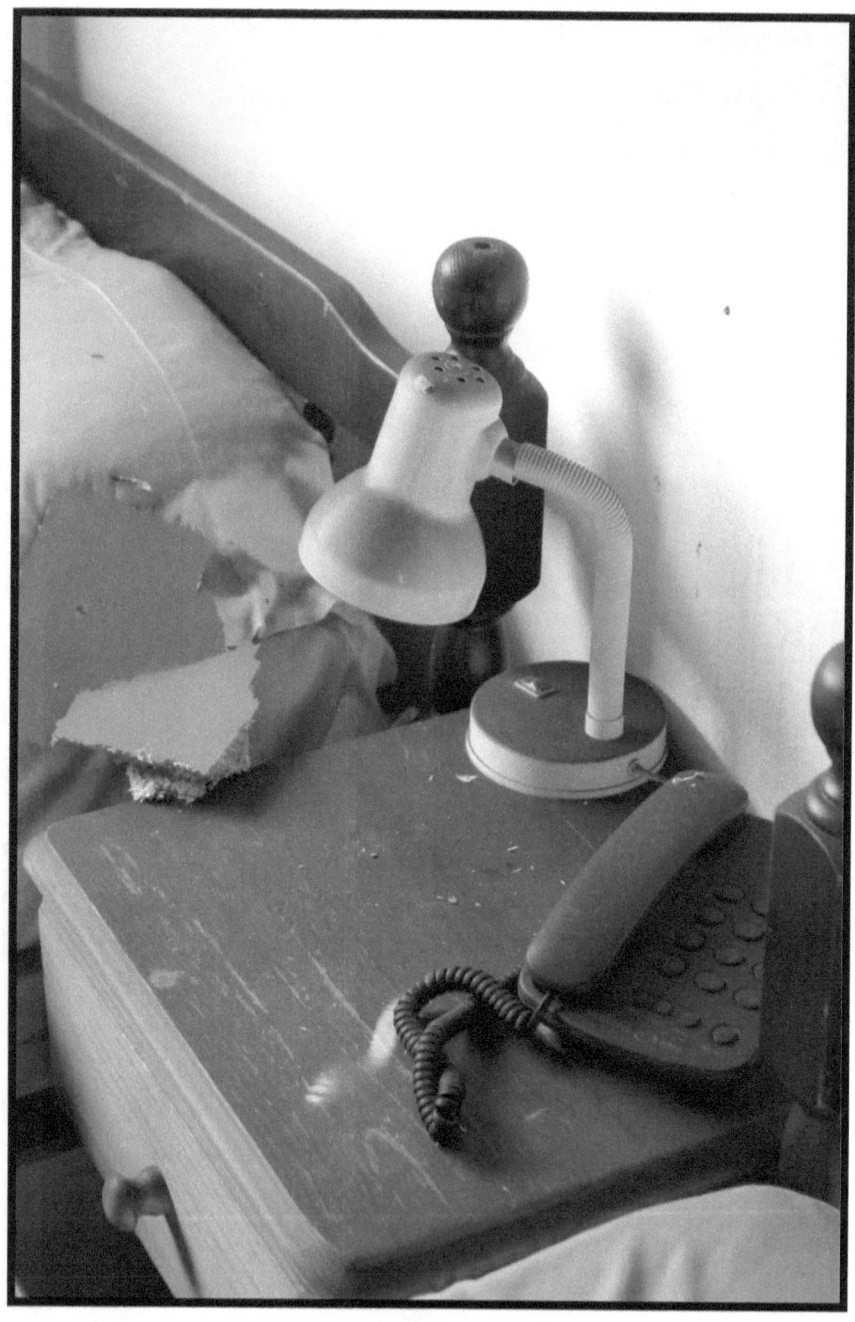

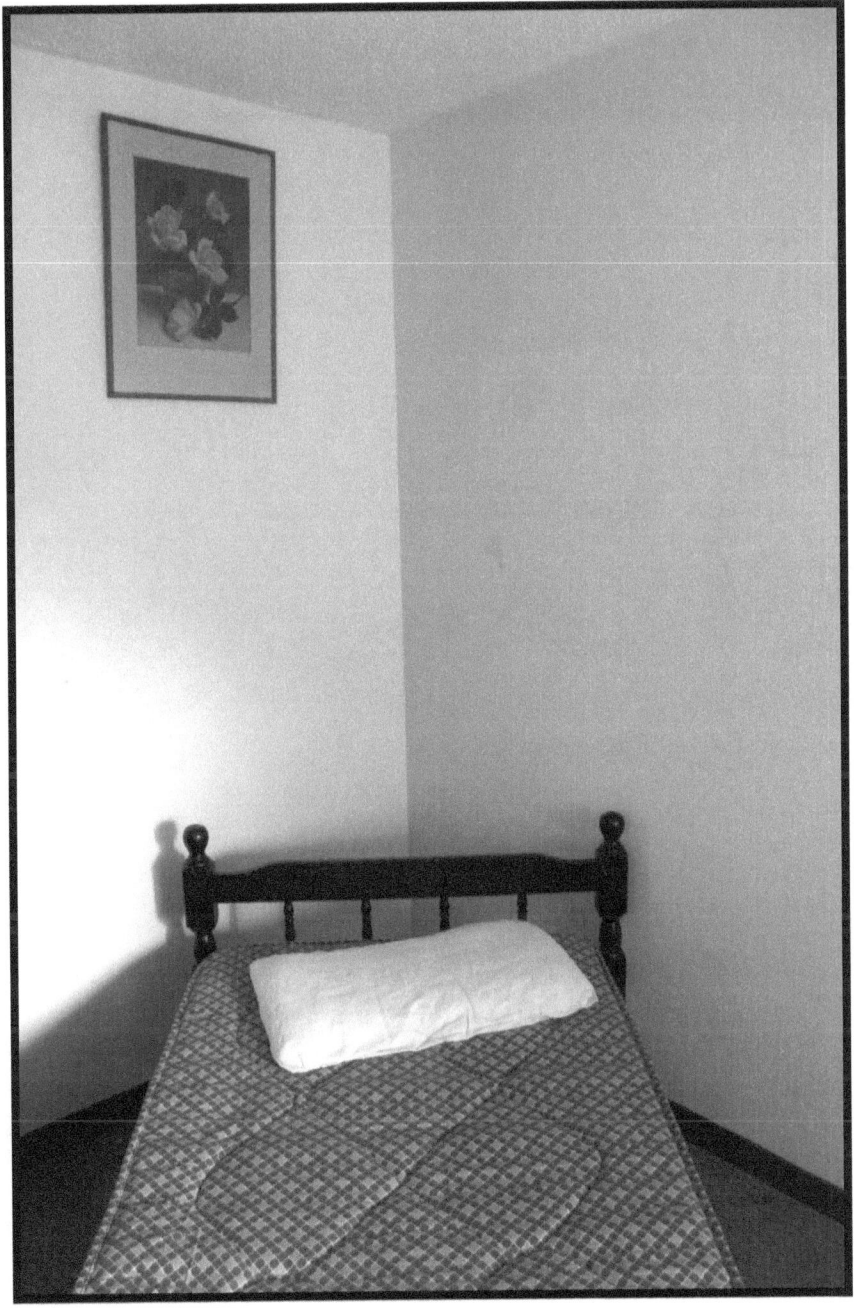

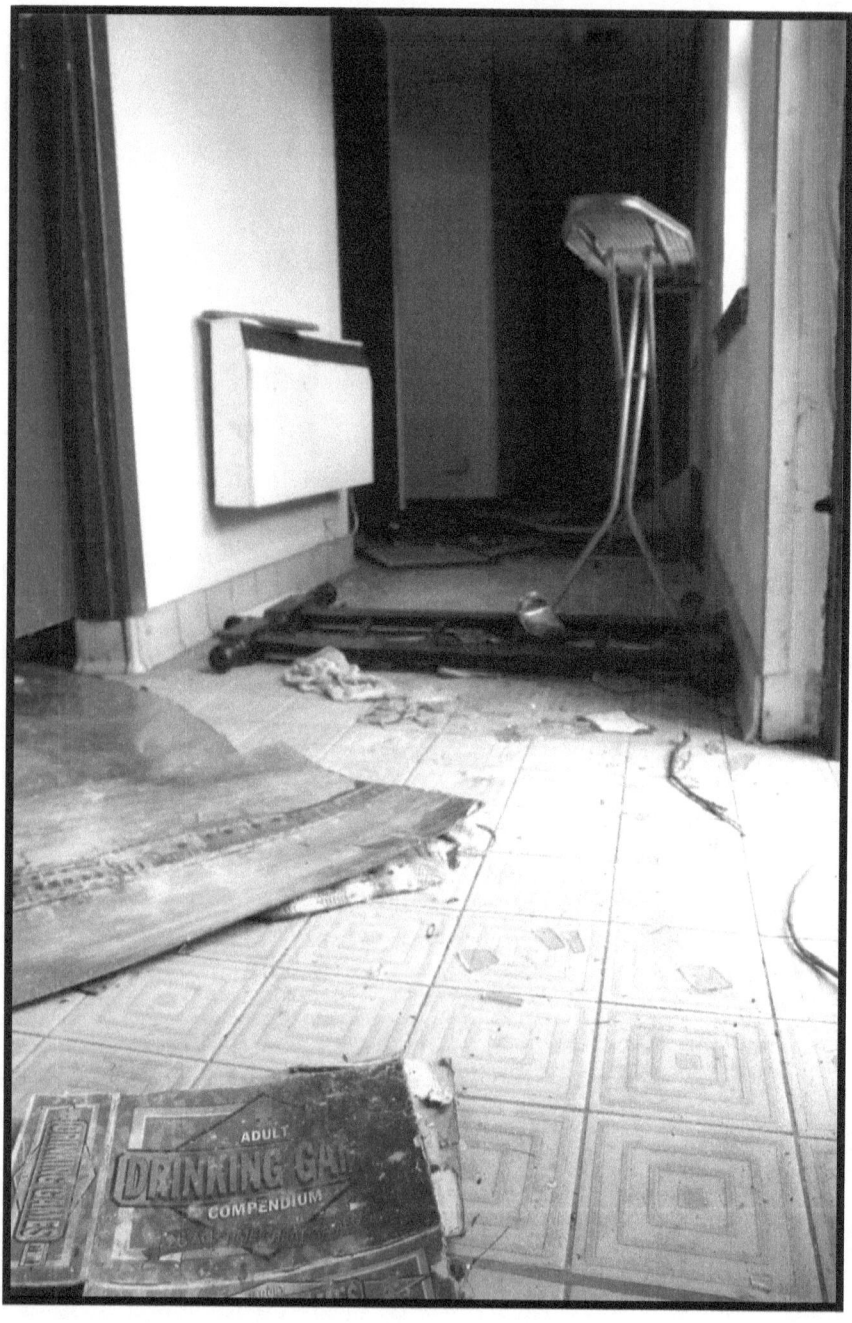

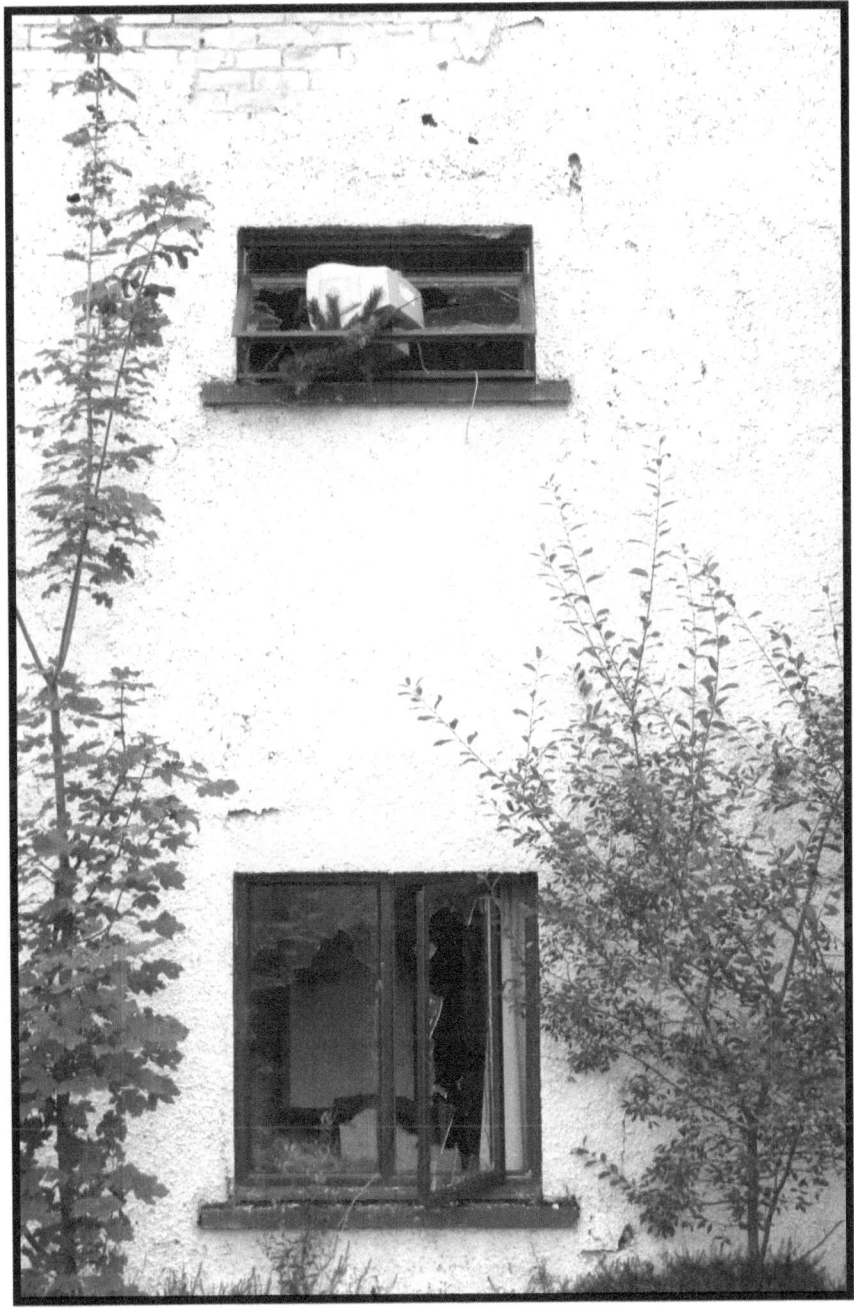

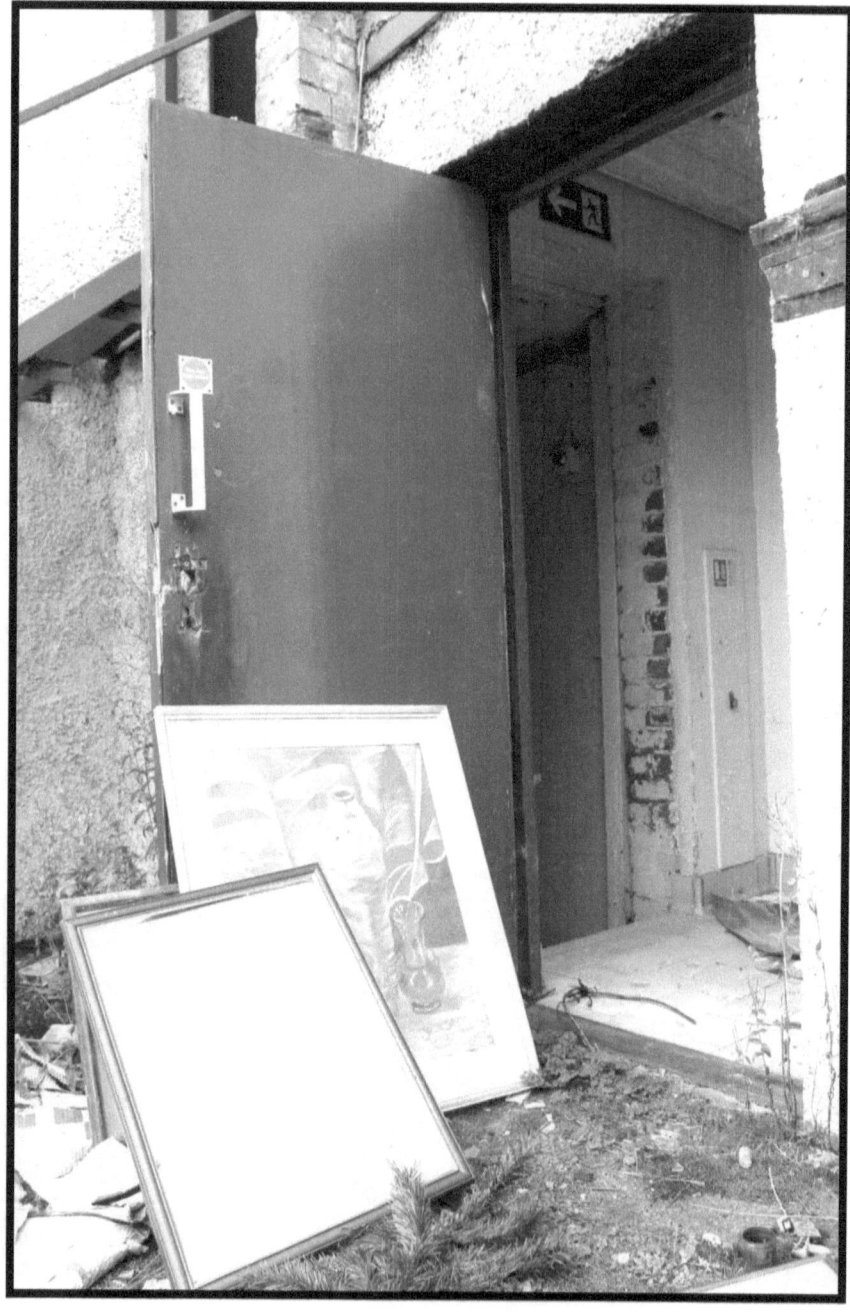

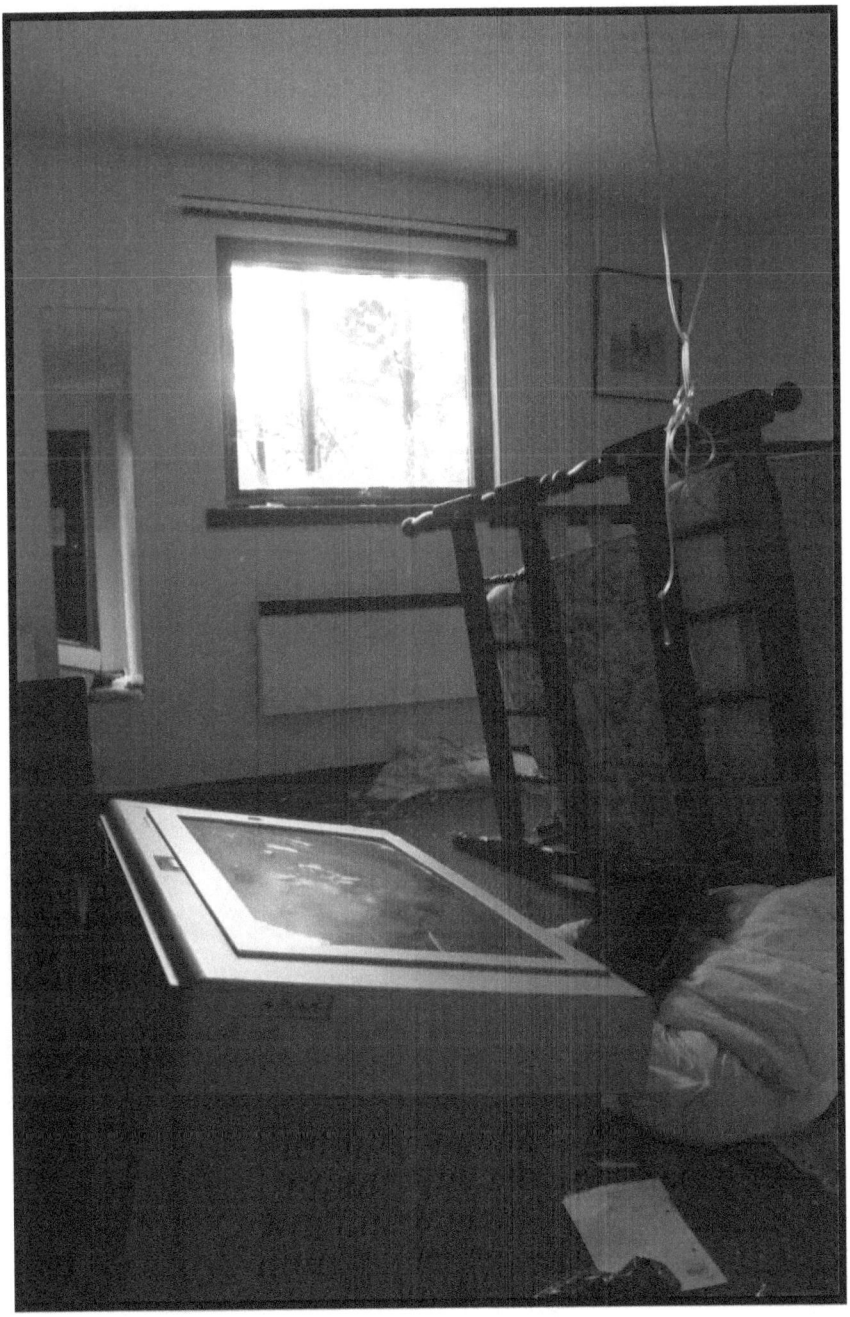

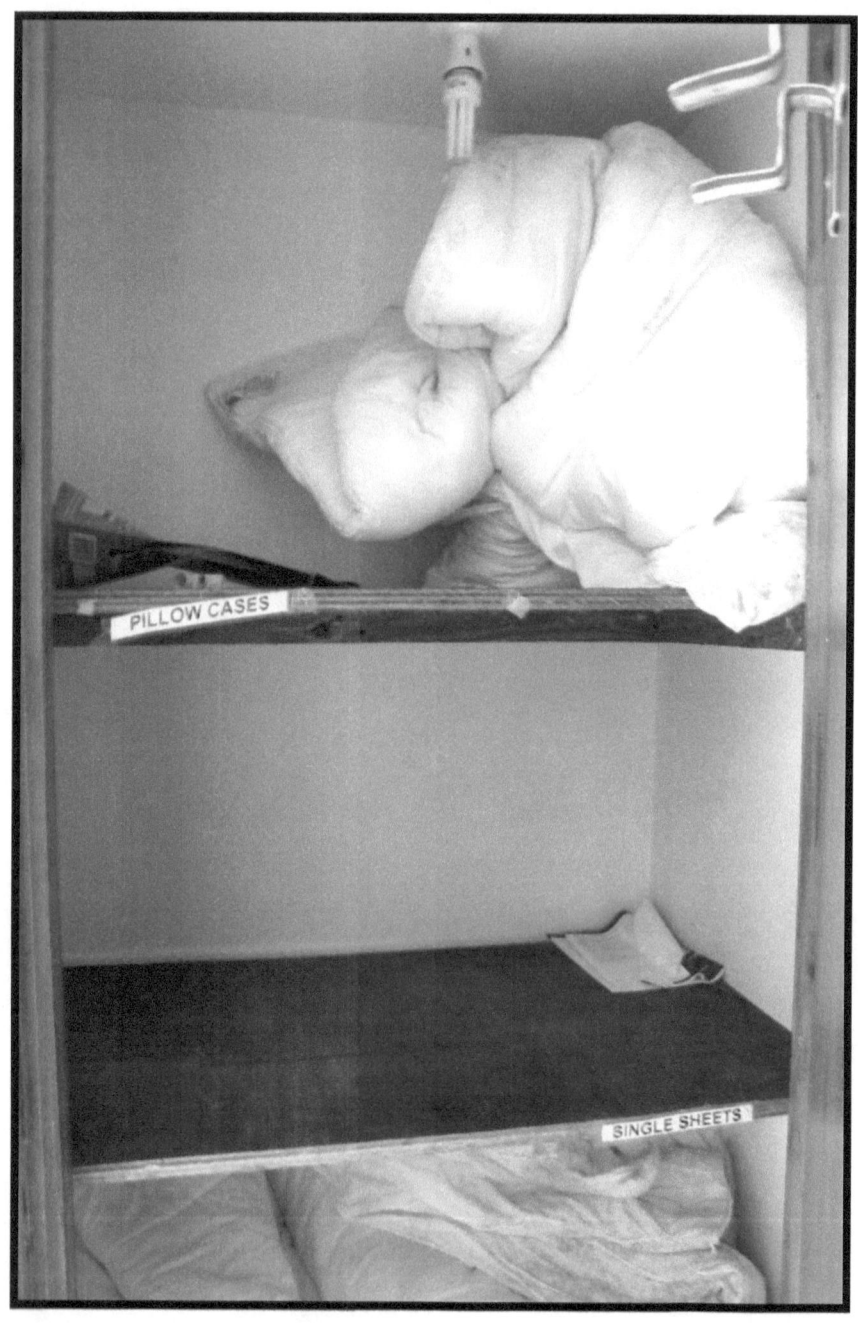

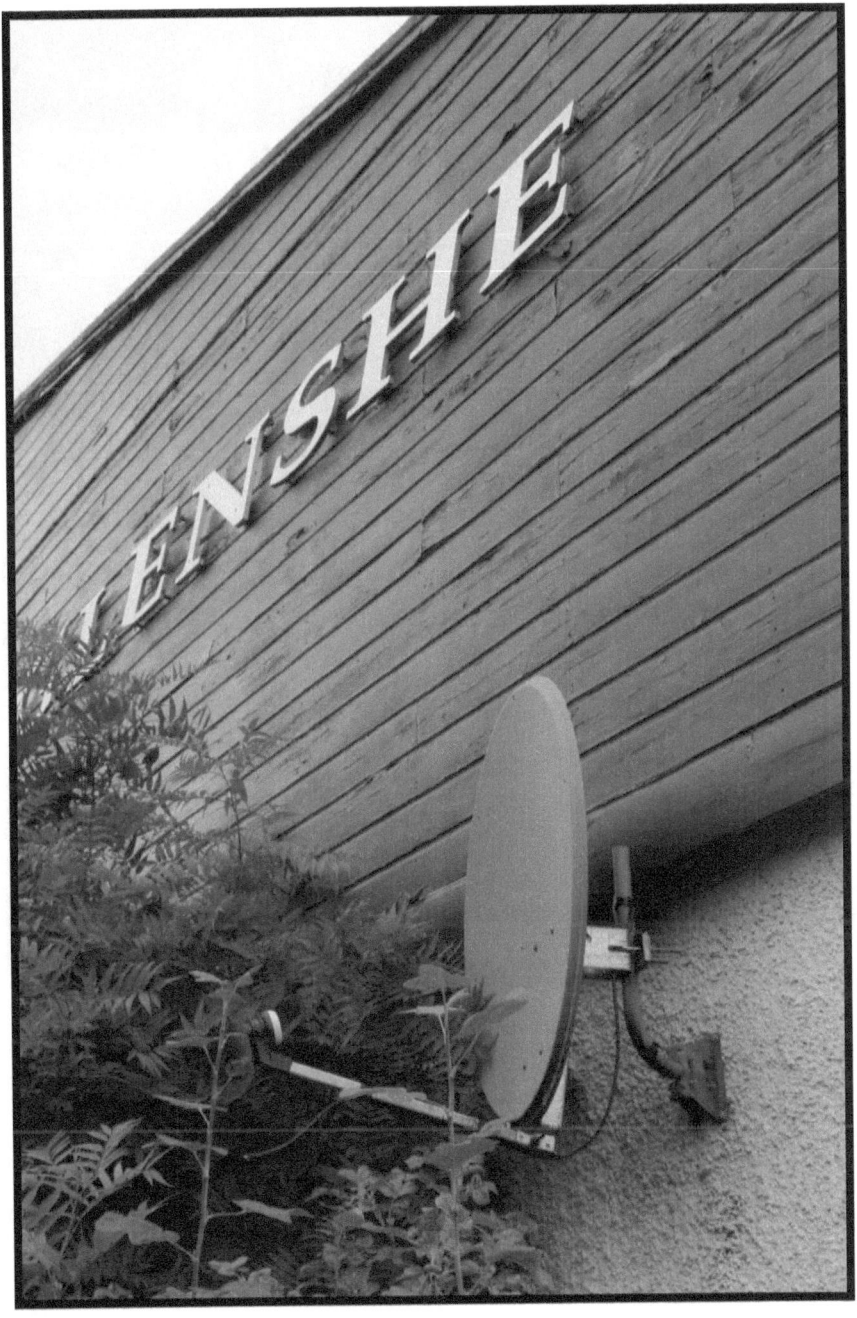

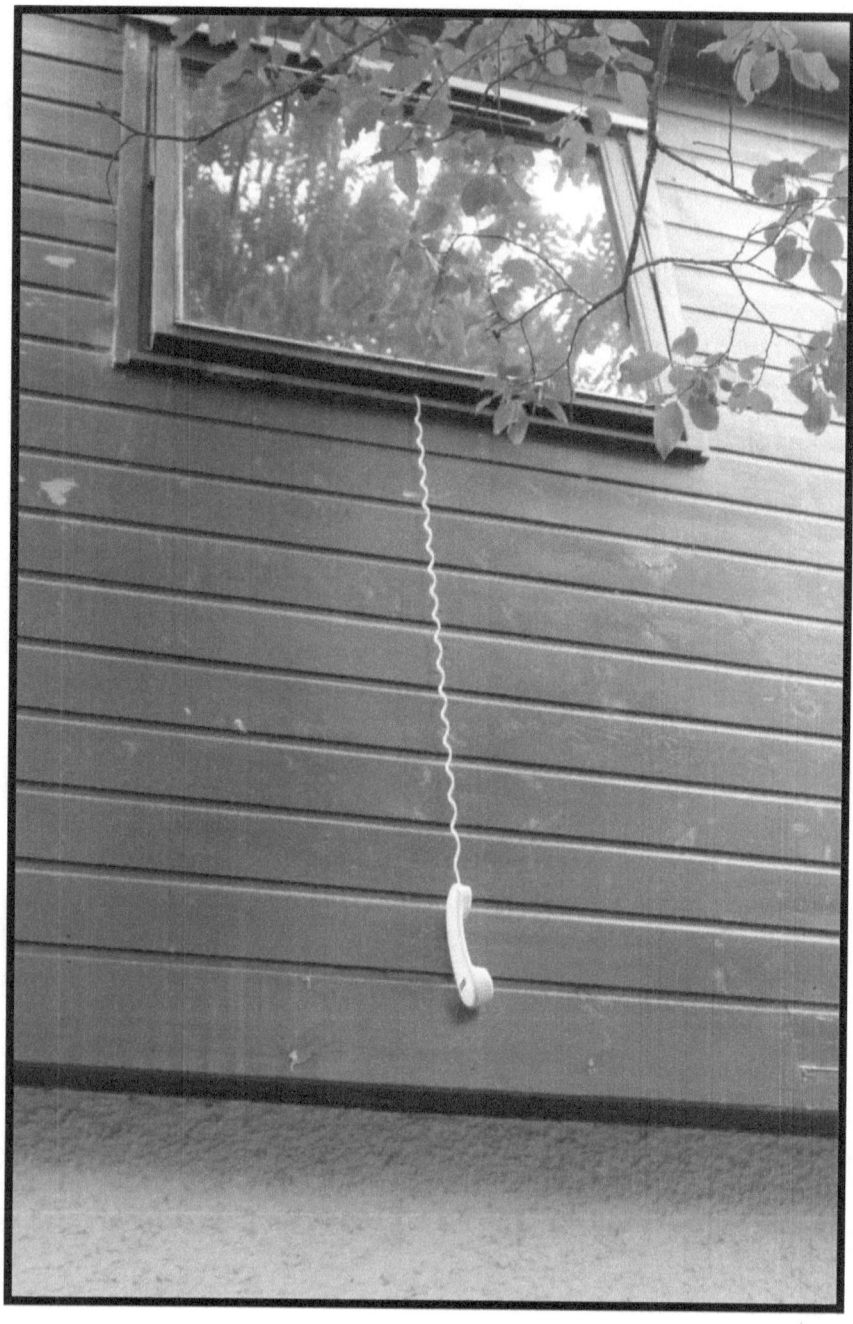

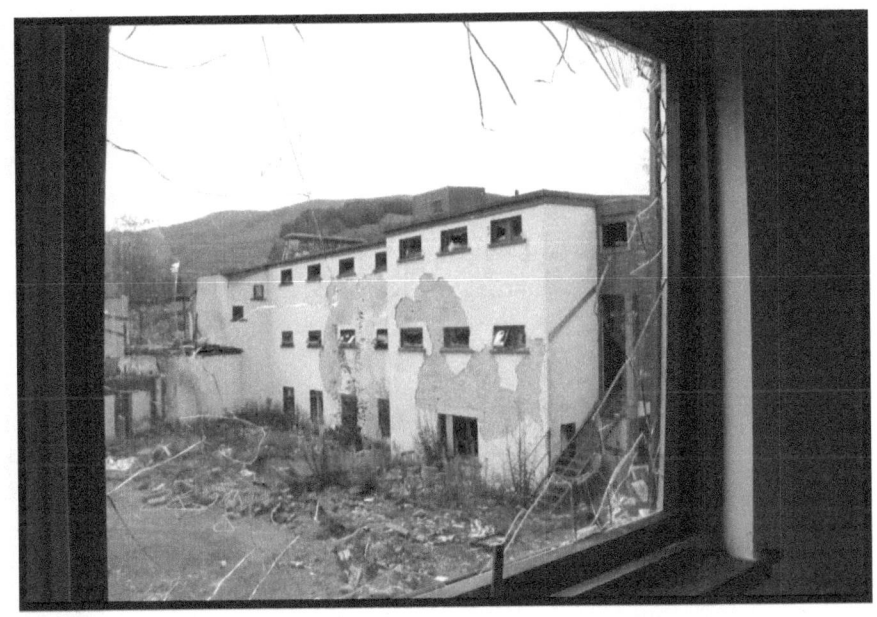

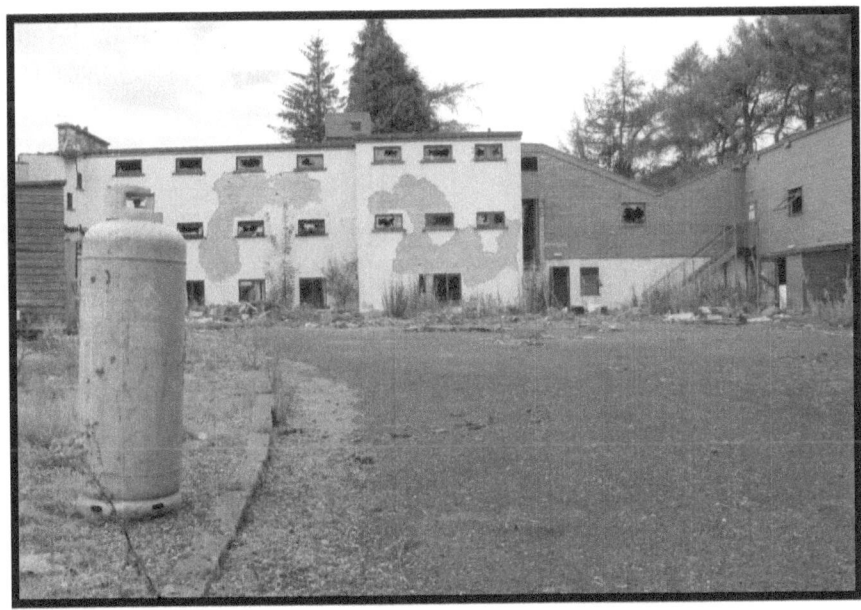

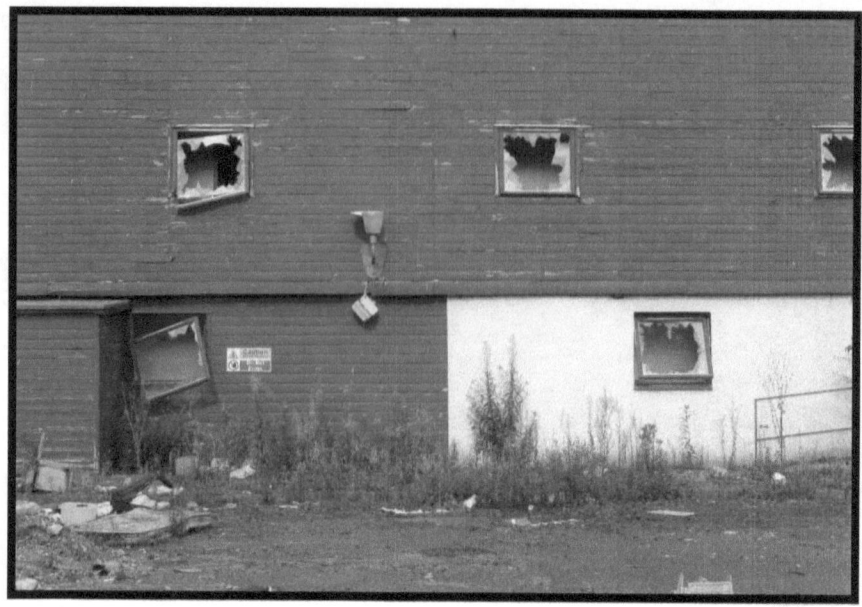

With the three-acre site becoming increasingly dilapidated, local residents formed the Spittal of Glenshee Project in 2015, hiring a firm of consultants to look at future uses for the land.

In August 2017, an outline planning application was lodged with Perth & Kinross Council by Yorsipp Ltd for the erection of a reception, bar and restaurant building, 18 holiday lodges, car parking and landscaping.

Acknowledgements

The following organisations and individuals are acknowledged as sources of images and information used with grateful thanks.

Mount Blair Community Archive

The Courier

Blairgowrie Advertiser

BBC News

Perth & Kinross Council

Spittal of Glenshee Project

Images are by the author or from the author's postcard collection with the exception of Mount Blair Community Archive, page 7 (bottom), page 9, 10 and 11; Dennis Winton, page 12 (top and bottom); Maggie Burke, page 16 (top and bottom); and BBC News, page 38.

Contemporary reviews sourced from Travel Republic and TripAdvisor Inc

Other Books by James Carron

Bothies, Huts & Howffs in the Hills: Perthshire & Angus

amenta.ink

Bothies are basic shelters in remote corners of the countryside, a home from home in the hills for walkers, backpackers, mountain bikers and others who love spending time in the great outdoors.

Scotland has a long tradition of 'bothying' and, while the better known ones are easily found, one of the great pleasures of exploring the nation's mountains and glens is stumbling upon one for the first time - and finding the door open.

This guide takes some of the guesswork out of the equation, listing unlocked habitable shelters, ranging from comfortable, well-equipped bothies suitable for overnight stays to simple wooden huts and howffs offering protection from the elements, a place to break for lunch or a bolthole in an emergency.

Covering Perthshire and Angus, the fully illustrated guide details the location of each bothy, hut or howff by grid reference, offers advice on how to reach it and outlines what to expect upon arrival.

For more information on Amenta Publishing titles, available in both ebook and paperback formats, please visit www.amenta.ink.

Highland Hermit – The Remarkable Life of James McRory Smith

amenta.ink

James McRory Smith lived for over 30 years at Strathchailleach, one of the most remote cottages in the Britain Isles. The building sits alone in a vast tract of empty, featureless terrain to the south of Cape Wrath, in Sutherland. There is no access road, no running water, no electricity and no telephone.

Yet James McRory Smith survived here, battered by the elements and devoid of human company. His story is a fascinating account of a man pitting his wits against the wilderness, enduring endless isolation and existing, for a large part, off the land. James' lifestyle belonged to a bygone age, yet he lived it in the 20th century, turning his back on the luxuries and conveniences of the modern world.

This biography provides readers with an inspiring account of a modern day hermit. It offers a rare insight into an alternative way of life, one that is far removed from the norm.

At a time when people are becoming increasingly concerned about consumption and consumerism, and their impact on the environment, James McRory Smith's story demonstrates the practicalities and challenges of the frugal, self-sufficient lifestyle many people dream of. However, this is not intended simply as a social history, is also a true-life story of adventure and survival.

For more information on Amenta Publishing titles, available in both ebook and paperback formats, please visit www.amenta.ink.

Tin Tabernacles and other Corrugated Iron Buildings in Scotland

amenta.ink

Corrugated iron is a common sight in industrial and agricultural buildings. Less common are the tin tabernacles, mission halls, hospitals, schools, houses and cottages constructed during the 19th and early 20th centuries. Derided by some, overlooked by others, those that remain standing to this day are legacy to a branch of architecture that dared to be different. Born of necessity, this black sheep of the building trade matured into a distinctive and delightful character of both the rural and urban landscape. Charting the history of corrugated iron as a construction material from its earliest days in the 1830s through to the Second World War, this book explores the once thriving market for kit-built kirks, ready to assemble reading rooms and off-the-shelf schools that sprung up across Scotland, often in some of the most remote and far flung corners of the country. Inexpensive to erect and frequently regarded as a temporary fix, many of these quirky little buildings remain standing and in use to this day.

For more information on Amenta Publishing titles, available in both ebook and paperback formats, please visit www.amenta.ink.

www.ingramcontent.com/pod-product-compliance
Lightning Source LLC
Chambersburg PA
CBHW031541210526
45464CB00003B/1101